Flaws of Oblivion

Flaws of Oblivion

An anthology for the Hippocrene Society

Edited by Devon Pearse & James Wilson

The Hippocrene Society
Neverland Publishing
2015

The Hippocrene Society
An imprint of Neverland Pubishing
2015

Printed in the United States of America
ISBN 13:
978-0-9888290-39
www.neverlandpublishing.com

Contents

Plamen Chetelyazov—*The Vignettes Collection*

Devon Pearse & James Wilson—*divertissements*

Virginia Goebel—*Poems*

Cary Polkovitz—*Often Overlooked*

About the Contributors

Introduction

I t was the first day of tenth grade. We entered the English classroom each with our preconceived notions and internalized concepts of what we were about to face within its walls, only to have all assumptions shattered and cast free upon the wind. Our desks stood not in straight and tiresome lines, but awaited us instead in a sort of makeshift circle, strewn about the room in an almost haphazard way. In the center of the circle of desks there moved a most unlikely authority figure. His sun-bleached hair swept nearly to his shoulders, his wild blue eyes assaulted us with interest, one by one. Upon the floor, also within the circle, he had placed, and was still placing, many photographs ripped from the pages of magazines or books or any other places one could think to find a photo. They were of Paris, hot air balloons, fruit, a waterfall, a forest, the seashore, the sunrise, a field of wild flowers. These pictures overlapped and formed a collage right there on the classroom floor. We stepped upon them gingerly, making our tiptoed way to our seats, wherever we could find one.

"Choose a photo," our teacher said once we had each selected a desk and made ourselves comfortable. "You can pick the first one you see, or the one closest to you… or you can decide which one makes you feel something. But know this—whichever one you choose, you must write something about it. And it must make me feel something."

And so began the year I became obsessed with poetry. Not only poetry for the sake of rhyme, but the idea of the poets in and of themselves. The ones who make their words to flow like water, who can create an image in another person's mind, touch another person's soul. The thoughts of writers and their readers mingle and entwine. Now other heights and chasms of the mind can be explored, new adventures can be shared, and we thus become immortalized through writing.

Alfred, Lord Tennyson observed, "I am a part of all that I have met." I agree, and am honored to share the pages of this book with a few dear friends and fellow writers of poetry and prose. We want to share ourselves with you, through our imaginings, heartbreaks, hopes, fantasies, dreams, and written words. Here is everything we are upon a page.

Here is what we've written. We hope it makes you feel something.

DP

We are haunted by what we want to forget, whilst what we want to remember fades slowly and incompletely away.

All too often writing is both an act of remembrance and an act of forgetting; and all too often it is unsuccessful on both of these fronts. In fact it is damned to be so.

When impelled to write out of a longing to project, expunge, emit and forget, one only ends up recording, prolonging and preserving that which one wants to cast out forever. (Inadvertently, one can even make heroes and virtues out of objects born of contempt.)

Conversely, when impelled to write out of a need to pass on, safeguard and cherish memories and feelings, one only ends up clouding and distorting that which once was, but which can never now be again (in quite the same way); and one only ends up frustrated by our boundless languages' ultimate limitations in refusing to ever truly render experience common.

There is, as such, a glorious failure in language, in every jot and tittle scribbled, in every syllable stuttered. And I hope this volume is a celebration of that failure.

In poetry, prose, and pieces that fall somewhere betwixt the two (not to mention some photography), we have in *Flaws of Oblivion* an anthology preoccupied with the problematics of remembrance and forgetting (and, inevitably, with the problematics of their conveyance by language also).

The lines of Devon Pearse's poems are sprinkled with souvenirs that turn into phantoms and phantoms that become souvenirs; my own brief "Skimming stones" seek both to sink and to ripple; our *divertissements* may claim to be diversionary, but distraction only ever follows (and is only ever followed by) reflection. Plamen Chetelyazov's "Vignettes," meanwhile, simultaneously document and banish the subjects they scrutinize, whether it be with affection or acerbity; the verse of Virginia Goebel is voiced by witnesses torn between disappearance and revelation; and Cary Polkovitz's short prose pieces are encomiums and eulogies to the neglected, abandoned and unheralded furnishings that lie about the metaphorical and literal sidewalks of our lives, just waiting for the reanimating breath of the imagination.

It is hoped that *Flaws of Oblivion* will be the first in a series of volumes to appear under the aegis of The Hippocrene Society, showcasing new writing and new writers from the broader stable of Neverland Publishing's ever-growing roster of talent, but even if it stands alone, a monument to its own disregard, it will have been worthwhile.

It is appropriate that I finish by not forgetting to thank the contributors and also expressing gratitude to Donna Font, Joe Font and Maggie Hawthorne of Neverland Publishing for all their fine work.

JW

Flaws of Oblivion

Devon Pearse
Selected Poems

Intramural

Only time is timeless, forever never comes
Tomorrow hasn't ventured out this far
Blinking just like fireflies who dance upon the night
These instances of grace kept in a jar

This cigar box in my mind is filled with useless souvenirs
Each cubbyhole is stuffed with wanton dreams
And the worn-out illusions of a misspent happenstance
The echoes come and go whene'er they please

Muses loll in sleepy doorways, shadows pattern every wall
Infused with threadbare colors of regret
Fervent light through wall-less windows and a fluid lullaby
That spent the night upon my window ledge

Through my flawless imperceptions of relentless quietude
The sand falls to the bottom of the glass
And though I play the cuckold and pretend I didn't see
Each grain becomes a portent of the past

Framed within the looking glass, cradled on the wind
Billowing from every broken pane
Lacy cobwebs, faded ink and other dusty things
What may have been or may still be again

Abstract

Remnants of a melancholy night
With twisted features
Mingled with the hopes and tear-drained eyes
Of emptiness still waiting to be born

The artist with his brush
Decides my fate
A bleeding through, a wonderful demise of space and time
Make me more than truth could ever be

I am unformed
As you create me
Fashioning your love through pain and contrast, lending life
And a borrowed soul you never thought would feel

Make me all your sorrows
Breathe into me
Every lovely thing you're terrified to let another see—the
    dark, the ugly
Becoming beautifully distorted and set free

A part of you
Now broken, lost
And laid to rest inside reality unreal, so colorful and stark; a
    tragic peace
And yet somehow you know I understand

A silver box without a key
Painted in place and locked away
Where you believe my heart should dream to beat
Longing for your pure imagination

Colors melting into canvas
Turning nightmares into daydreams
Like the lingering embrace of something not quite meant to be
An echo of a thought we may have shared

One wish to turn a phrase
To catch a whisper
Or to glimpse a thread unspoken and unfinished
Floating there for you to pick it up

The damage is the same
To speak your words, or rather mine
One and alike as raging phantoms of unrest
Will tear apart this empathetic calm

How real am I to you?
Or you to me?
Do I resemble what you love or hate or fear to be discovered?
Could you love me even knowing all I am?

I am your expression
Trapped and longing
Wanting so to live, to touch, to be your realization
To tell you that you'll never be alone

Is this all there is?
A final stroke, a tear
A last adoring look as you turn, to never know, to leave me
    in your gallery
To be seen as just another work of art

Mistaken

Forgetful as I am
So fond of daydreamed wishes, reveries and starlight
Selective memory is ever my sure downfall
Wanting so to find you
To find me

Convincing as you are
An innocent in armor I believed I'd pierced right through
Imperfect imperfection before me for the taking
A way to understand
A new belief

I once thought we shared a song
Fragile, incomplete and somehow beautifully damaged
So akin to what we had become
Reminiscent before now
Familiar aches

And I listened through the rain
Beyond the doubts that beat upon the roof
Telling me their vast and bleak intentions
All the sorrowful remains
I could not face

One day you let me in
And showed me all your scars, your steadfast demons
They frightened me, but still I would not go
Would not have left you
Nor released your hand

I waited here instead
Thought soon you'd open up your palm, cast down your eyes
Impossible to not know what you held
So bittersweet and real
An only chance

I let you move me
Like wind to tide, like shadows to the light
So soft, so free, so effortless this dance
A longing to believe
To know I could

The words you spoke, your laughter
All the light within your eyes I took for truth
While you assumed it all for folly's sake
I never should have known
And never would

In all these things I was mistaken
Choosing to believe in all you said, your candied words
Trust, not pride, the wounded party in this sham
No selfish jealousy or such
Just simple grief

To know that all I'd felt
And all you'd caused my heart to hope for and to need
Was nothing more than my own choosing to partake
There never was
Some other part of me

The Favored

Center of attention
Knaves and would-be lovers tangle rapturously in words
That slip from her tongue in silken eloquence
A sweet cascade of wanton thought
All ears within this space entombed
Wait restlessly to hear her next remark
And breathless expectations hang in silence
All the more fulfilling for their pains
They wonder at this mortal who, so much unlike myself,
Can serve to them their hearts upon a tray
While yet they watch
So helplessly bemused by artful guile
Here I, the keeper of the peace with aching heart
Wish desperately to catch the falling crumbs
And form of them a way to learn this grace
To hold within my hands this thing elusive
This riddle that I've failed to understand
While all the while these words
Held captive in my mind
Begin to tremble with the need to be set free
"Look at me!"
"See me!"
"I'll never hurt you, tease you, leave you, break your heart!"
"I want only to be known and to be seen for who I am—
Held separate and apart, not part of her
To have something that is ever all my own

That cannot be distracted by the banter and the guise
To see me, and me alone—be mine, all mine
To fascinate, to love, to form a thought.
Is it really all too much to ask?"
Laughter bleeds back into my hearing
I look around at nothing that has changed
And all that is the same
Center of attention
So far away from me, so unconcerned
I am companion to the favored—nothing more
As still and calm I sit
In utter silence

Bleak

I want to run in the snow. To feel it, crisp and cold, beneath my feet. To taste it on my tongue, let it turn my cheeks to pink as it melts upon my skin. My face upturned towards the sky to watch the whiteness fall.

The barren trees hold shadows in their arms; perhaps the memory of leaves, or thoughts of spring they hoard to keep them warm. Thick clouds dip low to share their wealth with me. The incandescent haze of twilight poised and waiting for its time.

Frost was rumored once to have stopped by this place, lingered briefly in poetical repose, then, a short while later, penned his thoughts in some brave manner such as this. We are all turned cowards in the winter; huddled by fires, wrapped in woolen garments, clutching steaming cups in our cold and trembling hands. The birds fly south, their feathers insufficient ward against the numbing chill.

And yet it is the term I love; this continuance of wintry solitude. The romance of the cuddling close, holding mittened hands, running, laughing, throwing snowballs, being children once again. Home and hearth and holly, candles all aglow within the frosted windows, warmth and comfort waiting just inside each bewreathed door.

My back is to them now, these initiates of cheer. Into the woods I ramble—seeking nothing more than silence and an untouched drift of snow. A fallen log to sit upon, an anchor in this endless tide of white. Every tree is sketched bemusedly upon a stark and pristine canvas. A trembling leaf still clings to what she knows. Then, with unabashed spontaneity, abandons her last purchase, forgetting why she waited for so long. Twisting, pirouetting, through the nipping, flake-filled air. As though she finally believes this avocation might be fun.

What daring I have witnessed in this quaint, untrodden place. If only I could have such nerve as she!

Me, Tonight

My heart beats like a whisper. A memory of something old and dear. The miracle of childhood like the promise of the rain, or the first day of summer, or the way the grass smelled with the sunshine upon its back. All things come and go. I watched the tide recede and chase itself back home again. Greedily it raked the shore, trying to catch hold of something to take with it. Some things it can and some it never could. So like me, this urgency it renders. A lullaby for the always-restless and unkempt.

The sunset was behind me, but I glimpsed its sweet refraction in the waves. The frailty of evanescing light. A pool of thought beside me, an undertow that echoes through my veins. The sound of fading footfalls on the boardwalk. Time stands here alone. The revelation was humbling and it followed me home.

Now I stare at my reflection without ripples and I miss their company—the character they bring. I still smell of the ocean and the day. My hair is soft and filled with salt, mixed strands of pale and gold. My eyes still haunted by the sea. They are emeralds in my skin, like the shells upon the sand. I am so comfortably replete, drained of everything but ponderings and hope. There is something that I recognize. I smile at the freckles on my nose. I am still me.

The cries of the gulls will carry me to sleep and I will dream of flying with them over water, over dunes, over all of life that seems so small below. A little girl with wispy hair who dances in the rain, who runs along the sand and drives the waves to join her. Who picks the wild flowers and entwines them in her tresses. Who believes in magic seashells and mermaids and waits for Peter Pan.

The waves still know her name. It is the same as mine. She leans close to me, tan skin, pink lips and laughing eyes. Nearly caught upon the wind, like a memory of breath, so real then gone, she whispers through sheer curtains. "I'm still here."

Creed

There is no disgrace in shades of absolutes
The key to aimless reckonings lies deep inside the chasm of
    your mind
Arise and leave this place to mortal souls who seek
Yellow and green consistencies in all surrounding thoughts
Did you see Forever as she ventured past your door?
Like a bucket full of fireflies, held fast within her grasp
Insistent, this need to fulfill the unfulfilled; to light the
    darkened road
Aggravation's innovation of tomorrow, things unsaid and yet
    undone
Somewhere left of desire is an empty space of lonely little
    dreams
Sincerity's subtle veil rent asunder by the deeper truth of pain
Conciliatory expressions of forget-me-nots and follow-
    throughs of shame
Oblivion awaits beyond my heart's demise
Ride across these pale skies of ecstasy, sewn through with
    tattered stars
Always lurking consciousness, the enemy of pure, exquisite self
Increasingly unreal indications of the sanity which hides
    within us all
There remains one choice to those who dwell as I
If you must live, live truly, poised to die

Inspiration, unexpected

I walked today a long, alluring path
This mesmerizing nothingness a contrast to the looming cliffs
    of doubt
Around me swayed the graceful frame of life

Oscillating theories dancing past me on the breeze,
Their blinded colorations never ceasing to inspire
Imperceptive passion is swept away to far-off shores

As a plausible coincidence becomes my dearest friend
The irascible pinhole of sardonic substructure opens
Like a cognitive sunflower welcoming the light

And placid repression of self becomes the worn-out
    grappling hook
Of so much exalted oil

One Day

Upon the illusory One Day

I'll find myself alive and yearn to breathe,
To daydream on a pillow made of clouds

I'll watch the angels of the dust motes
That spiral in the seamless rays of light
Far beyond the understanding of their human counterparts

A wish to play on old remembrances
As shadows play on sight and hollow dreams

I'll forge my own forget-me-not... one day

Perseids

I went to watch the stars fall, that I might believe again
In the soaring of the spirit and the calling of the wind
Yet my soul did rest uneasy, feeling tethered to the land
My feet more prone to wander as they trod upon the sand

I went to watch the stars fall, with the yearning that I might
Somehow recall the bliss of childhood in the fading of each light
But I saw not one sweet memory, shed not a single tear
No angel sang the lullaby I had so hoped to hear

I went to watch the stars fall, hoping you would join me there
For the moonlight sweetly beckoned and the sea was calm
        and fair
Hope was my lone companion on this scenic Lover's Night
And she, too, departed with the coming of the light

I went to watch the stars fall, to find myself once more
In the company of solitude upon a lonely shore
Ever after shall I linger here, for here I have come home
To see the stars gaze down upon me and to watch them
        fall… alone

Residual

"Am I strong enough for this?" she thought
Gazing through the fabric of her dreams
So many wounded hours spent before herself
In renderings of doubt

Belief is the true catalyst of change
Momentum gained from following one thought
Which leads to others intertwined
Within a broken window of the soul that yearns to breathe

Solitude is solace
For a time the only voice
That moves the sweet breeze of regret
Through memories and heartache and the need to set them
    free

The Blushing Moon

Wait for me—I'll follow soon, underneath the Blushing Moon
Where the boldest lovers swoon, here beneath the stars
Call to me—I'll come to you, pleading with the Blushing
    Moon
Love's impatience in full bloom, my heart knows where you are

Take my hand—as e'er you do, we'll pass under the Blushing
    Moon
To be reborn as creatures new upon the other side
Hold me close—your love to prove, in the red-glow of the
    Blushing Moon
All passions of the heart pursued to the rhythm of the tide

Dry my tears—may they be few, that spill before the
    Blushing Moon
This memory of love entombed within my shadowed heart
Bid me farewell—a fond adieu, our time beneath the
    Blushing Moon
But all too brief—you fade from view as ever we must part
Eclipse…

Anamchara

Let's sing together
On this weary road
Let's tumble and embrace
And knock each other down
To start again

Let's wear each other out
Like a pair of old shoes
Remember how it feels
To pound the pavement
But always together

Soles and souls worn thin
But somehow worn just right
The dust of morning settles
On the stream we follow
Through the woods of time

To reach the branches
Seemed a daunting task
Until you held my hand
And then the climbing
Wasn't very hard

And letting go was easier
Than either of us dreamed that it could be
Just let your fingers slip
And know that I will follow
With a smile

James Wilson
Skimming stones

Positively stone

thinking positively or just not thinking at all
cowardly seconds disappear until
the times
cherish
○

Lingering stone

i appear in the background of your photos
for now and always
is it
that
○

❧ FLAWS OF OBLIVION

Slur stone

just what does love mean to you anyway?
one player goads another
an audience
forever
○

Molière stone

my french failing me again with unexpected consequences
she left me alone
after that
infamy
O

Ex stone

a window on a screen prompting her friendship
years, love, hatred, sex
all ignored
possibilities
O

Numb stone

---

sever my cingulate gyrus; have done with it
all feelings are pains
knowledge means
absolute
○

Searing stone

have you seen the cruelty in their eyes?
flashing like lizard tongues
hating us
innocents
○

Antinomy stone

the archaic belief systems that won't go away
both torture and comfort
all here
inevitably
O

Influx stone

people cry out, jimbo, what's wrong with humanity?
flick the switch now
i reply
damn
○

Speed stone

i.m. G.S.

that shameful curiosity when someone's taken too soon
autumn sun shining bright
featherless flight
beyond
O

Medecine stone

here comes the doctor prescribing placebos and potions
fluctuation between two extremities:
love and
pointlessness
○

Library stone

reflected in the cabinet windows beyond dusty spines
look there, our faces
gaining pallor
fast
○

Philosopher's stone

failing, fading, but never, it seems, disappearing entirely
a quality almost nameless
for centuries
now
○

Belonging stone

from the shimmering heights to the spectral wants
beneath night blue skies
a homeland
awaiting
○

X-ray stone

---

and now he's in love with the world
he finally saw beyond
suits, styrofoam
sycophancy
○

Radiant stone

---

atop these vast waters that never become familiar
for what it's worth
i'm pure
love
○

Plamen Chetelyazov
The Vignettes Collection

The Hills of Plovdiv[1]

Gloomy, rainy and fresh—my favorite weather…

It had been drizzling softly and continuously for days.

Then the sun came and with its fiery kisses life blossomed.

I like it when the smell of spring overpowers the smell of dog shit.[2] I like it in late April when I lie on the wet grass somewhere up in the hills.[3] Usually I stare aimlessly at the stars until the evening chill drains the alcoholic intoxication from my burning body. Sometimes, when I'm less drunk, I remember the hundreds of used syringes scattered all around and the diseases that lurk in the cold and thirsty needles, keening to prick some unsuspecting soul. Alternatively, immersed in the sobriety of a judge, I think of the kids who quite deliberately stick those same cold needles into their veins—the children who every night mix up greedy, synthetic oblivion with their own dear blood.

Right now I am soaked and prostrate on the grass watching my cigarette smoke; noticing how the smoke always dissolves before it can touch the stars. Too far away… But it is OK. So slow, calm and beautiful. The huge moon and its silver spray are painting brilliant cobwebs on the grass, on the ivy, and upon the leaves of the trees. The birds' songs are mixed with the muted rumble of the town. And all my dreams are hidden from the vanity of others and my own complexes too.

Is it happiness? Or freedom?

…Whatever. It works.

[1] An extract from Plamen's first novel, *Параноя (Paranoia)* (Varna: LiterNet, 2007).

[2] The streets of Bulgaria teem with a huge population of stray and abandoned dogs and the country has the highest number of taenia infections in the European Union.

[3] Plovdiv, the second largest city in Bulgaria, is built upon seven syenite hills, three of which are declared sites of architectural preservation, three more as natural landmarks, whilst the last one has been destroyed by a proliferation of paving stones.

Self-determination[1]

The earliest childhood memories are woven by shadows. And some of these shadows are woven from fire. I kept the clearest of them in the drawers of my dreams for a long long time. And when I slept they sent me back to the town of Ivaylovgrad.

Against my parents' wishes, we moved to my mother's birthplace when I was 3 years old. The year was 1985 and Socialism was in full bloom, its insanity consuming peoples' lives just as the ruthlessness and greed of certain goons continues to consume lives today. Ivaylovgrad is a small town on the south side of the Rhodope Mountains, a place where summer whispers to winter and where the breath of the Mediterranean ruffles the shaggy slopes of Orpheus' peaks. Ivaylovgrad is a magical place. At least for me it is, though plenty of others will curse it for its contrasting populations of young street urchins and very old men.

The young people in this town seem to immediately and imperceptibly collapse into old age and dotage. The good taste the beginning of man's circle of life and they sip from the emotions of lost innocence until they just wither in utopia like Delopolyane's shriveled mulberries in late summer.[2] The bad, meanwhile, sink into a dotage where they are immune from such emotions, thinking only about mischief. They drink, cheat and fight all day long because there is nothing else to do. And so, in Ivaylovgrad, the people are either very old or just kids.

The grandmothers grow potted lemon trees on the stairs of the old brick apartment blocks—buildings with black asphalt roofs and basements smelling of wine barrels. And the grandfathers, well, they lazily sprawl their stiff bodies on benches placed in the shadows of the pomegranates, sipping thoughtfully from homemade *rakia*, their walking sticks resting beside them.

And the kids, not those failing mischievous adults, but the real children... Well, for them, Ivaylovgrad is a paradise, a Wonderland. A place at which the worms of time have been nibbling, creating huge holes, entire passageways between dimensions, tunnels through which the local kittens, truly magical creatures, boldly lead the kids, moving from place to place, and from time to time. The leaves of the town's fig trees curl up with the sound of the fresh-voiced youngsters, then, barely a minute later, the same sounds are out there on the slopes, engulfed in the sticky scent of the resin. Their radiant laughter bathes in the waters of the river Arda, afterwards flying off with the wind and out across the steppes, close to the ruins of the ancient villa Armira.[3] And if you go by the vineyards, you can see Greece, a land where white cottages are scattered in amongst the burnt stubble. I sometimes wonder what our adobe houses look like from over there... I wonder if the Greeks even look at them at all. But, irregardless, I bet that the stars' scurf sprinkles just the same above them as it does above here. You see, when daylight drowses during the night, its dreams are projected in the sky over Ivaylovgrad.

This is how I remember the town. This is the place in my world. I guess the reality is quite different—a location languishing in an isolated area of a poor country, a village of limitations where nothing happens save the pressing and perennial playing out of the complexes of the locals. But I don't trust reality. She was the first to insult my ugliness.

It was back in my hometown of Plovdiv. I was 7 years old and the magic of Ivaylovgrad was far far away and unable to protect me. Maybe that old armoire was also to blame—a dark cyclops, a butler that continues to loom by the front door of my parents' flat with an unblinking mirrored eye. Now, of course, I miss this armoire, but not back then. I used to stand before its mirrored eye and I didn't like what I could see. Perhaps this was the birth of a complex inspiring the sluggish awakening of my ego and the first timid attempts of self-determination? Perhaps that was how it worked for me? For others the response might be completely different— one can imagine how the mirror is caressed by the crystal clear looks of innocent little girls with ribbons blue as irises woven into their sunny ringlets. Well, *you* can imagine it, it is too difficult a task for me. I was always knocked back by my reflection—it was so ugly that it annoyed me. And while some were observing their physical metamorphoses, marking their heights with scratches on the steam pipes, I was busy with the painful exercise of denying myself, although I was but a child and such deliberate a denial was impossible. Instead I chose to falsify the facts and, from that very young age, I have dedicated my life to a doomed struggle against reality and the things that cannot be otherwise.

1   An extract from Plamen's first novel, Параноя (*Paranoia*) (Varna: LiterNet, 2007).

2   Belopolyane is a village in the municipality of Ivaylovgrad, southern Bulgaria.

3   Villa Armira is a 1st-century suburban Roman villa that lies some 4 kilometers southwest of Ivaylovgrad. The Villa was destroyed by the Goths in the late 4th century, around the time of the Battle of Adrianople in 378.

The Organ Grinder[1]

A gloomy workday's afternoon. Heavy electrified clouds hang over the Old Town of Plovdiv.[2] I am rambling along Syborna Street, moving towards Sts Constantine and Helena Church. I know that there, in front of the temple, leaning carelessly on his heavy street organ, one can find Mr Dancho.

I remember this colorful old man from my childhood. He is always in the same place, embraced by the scent of the figs in the summer, and covered by the grayness of the clouds in the winter.

And there he is. The eighty-seven-year-old man recognizes me, greets me with a friendly wave. I photographed him some time ago and today I'm bringing the images with me. He looks at them, likes them, enjoys them with childlike pleasure. He decides to thank me with his art. And whilst he tunes the street organ, he babbles, explaining that the instrument cannot create music without soul.

Now everything is ready. The artist turns the handle and magic is flushed out from within the mechanical box. The sun throws the clouds wide open to enjoy it. The cats on the stone walls shake off their springtide's nap, sharpen their ears, and purr. The strangers drop their daily cares, problems rolling down the steep cobblestones and disappearing around the corner…

On 26th February, 2008, Uncle Dancho entered Plovdiv's memory forever. Another magical spark from the Three Hills' utopia that will always shine in our recollections.[3]

---

[1] First published in the Bulgarian newspaper *Anonce*, "The Organ Grinder" was then incorporated into the second edition of *Параноя* (*Paranoia*) (Smashwords, 2012).

[2] The Old Town, an autonomous area within the modern city of Plovdiv, features more than 150 monuments of culture and has been declared an architectural-historical reserve.

[3] The Old Town is situated on the so-called "three hills" formed of Nebet Hill, Dzhambaz Hill and Taksim Hill.

Do You Have a Light?[1]

So, you need a story? I'm your man! And from somewhere out of the chaos of letters born from the creative efforts to satisfy my fucking vanity I must find the phrase "Do you have a light?"

"What vanity?" do I hear you cry? Well, it's the self-same vanity that leads all the workers in your editorial office to kibitz for hours in the toilets, bent over their own brand-new published articles, sousing themselves with selfish ecstasy with each rereading. I think you know what I'm talking about.

Oh, but let's not be petty. Besides, I have a limit to my words.

Here is my story. It's coming into view, pushing aside the calm alcohol dizziness that has spilled through my consciousness. For a moment the subject fusses around my dreams, appearing in the interstices of my brain as small soap bubbles. But this is not a noble story, not like the tales I feed with my ideals. No, nothing like that. This is going to be a very dull story. A text that will bypass the noble impulses with an arrogant derision akin to that of a BNT artistic director walking impassively past a group of journalism students.[2]

My story begins in a Plovdiv bar, a place plunged in cigarette smoke and colored by a soothing neon light. Why? Because I am from Plovdiv—that's why! I am going to add a cold beer. Why not a bottle of whiskey? Because my story is cheap and cannot afford such props. Goddamn, even my imagination is not wealthy enough to order a bottle of Jack! But wait, let's see— four tequila shots would be ideal company for the doomed beer. Yeah… that's better. A painfully familiar environment. I'm talking about that masochistic pain discovered nightly only to be denied morningly. The denial depends on just how many tequila shots I'm going to pal up with that beer—you know which beer, the one that comes from a large family all living happily together in an attractive freezer near the bar. And today I'm quite friendly, I think. Hmm… I'm only writing about alcohol and already my story is going nowhere. Usually it's like this: I sit down and drink with the idea of clarifying just where I am going with my life, and then, after a while, I am unable even to stand on my feet…

Good, we have a bar, cigarette smoke, neon lights, a sufficient amount of money to cause the bored bartender to shuttle— bottle of tequila in hand—between the beer's familial home over there and my corner over here. So what music to play? Shit! No, it's not going to be *chalga*!³ Whose stupid idea was that? I do not want to listen to the soundtrack of a cheap soft-porn production! But what choice do I have? We are in Plovdiv… Here everything is *chalga* for fuck's sake! Well, you can hear decent live music at The Spot,⁴ but such a place is too close to my dreams… and I promised not to confuse my ideals with this schizophrenic outpouring created by my (still unacceptably sober) brain. And now I'm sounding like an advert for my favorite drinking den, so no doubt you won't publish this. I always screw everything up! My sister says it might be some kind of karma. And she says that with compassion. Anyway, so what if I screw up? It usually unshackles my stories.

I leave my imaginary jukebox to unleash a playlist. With great satisfaction I observe the loading of Massive Attack's "Butterfly

Caught," Cigaretta's "Ascetic," and "Woozy" by Faithless.[5] And that's it. The word count shows over 3000… And if time somehow corresponds to the number of words in my text, I have only a few minutes for a very short story and a very brief soundtrack. So I decide to play Ostava's "Stop" first and the others will have to form a queue and wait.[6] The utopian melancholy of the melody floods the brain banks, brimming over with a pleasant coolness, extinguishing the beer and the tequila that are burning in my esophagus and stomach.

I bet you think I'm some kind of jolly fellow. Well I'm not. I am a lonely, insignificant and totally hopeless depressive. I know it and that's why I'm drinking quietly at the bar.

And then… She appears. Everybody starts gazing in a trance. Her legs remind me of the sets of compasses we used to have in school. Sigmund Freud would understand such a strange analogy, I'm sure. Her short skirt and absurd vest are worn to emphasize rather than conceal her sexuality. The other guys gape at these assets with weak-minded and glazy stares. The black, straight hair contrasts with the pale face. A vampiric vision so impressive one would think twice about placing an order for garlic bread. Her eyes are crystal blue, like the eyes of the husky dogs I sometimes dream of. Those dogs chase me and I run all night before eventually grasping that they just want to play. And I swear that these beautiful blue eyes are fixed on me. She approaches with insouciance, setting a stinking cigarette between her exquisite lips. The bartender is no longer bored and watches intently and with envy as She stops by my bar chair. "Do you have a light?" She asks, stooping to reveal her low neckline and placing, as if by accident, her delicate palm on my knee… "No, I don't smoke! If you need a fucking light so badly you can get a box of matches from the goddamn liquor store near the bar's entrance! Stupid fool! Can't you see that I was listening to some good music, that this is my story and that the only things worth my attention are the tequila shots and the beer in front of me! You rotten slut!" I have not even delivered my speech to the shocked girl before the bartender, fast as a snake, has reached over with a lighter already aflame, lubberly spilling in the process my precious—the alcohol in which I was so deeply absorbed.

Sometimes women do spoil everything…

---

1 "Do You Have a Light?" was conceived for a Bulgarian lifestyle magazine's literary contest which had the stipulation that the question "Do you have a light?" feature in the text. The essay was later built into Plamen's second novel Имаго (Imago) (Smashwords, 2012).

2 Bulgarian National Television (BNT) is the public broadcaster of Bulgaria.

3 Chalga is the most popular music genre in Bulgaria. It is a blend of Turkish, Bulgarian, Arabic and Gypsy influences and deals openly with themes of sex and money. The genre is often criticized by Bulgarian intellectuals for a perceived tawdriness and a portrayal of loose morals in its lyrics and in the image of its singers.

4 Rorschach's Spot is a legendary night club in Plovdiv that was founded by Alexander Sekulov, one of the most famous contemporary writers in Bulgaria. It is a venue that holds many concerts and art performances.

5 "Butterfly Caught" is a song from Massive Attack's fourth album, 100th Window (2003). Cigaretta are an avant-garde band from Bulgaria and "Ascetic" is a song from their second album, Pluke (2006). Faithless's "Woozy" appears on the soundtrack to the film The Beach (2000).

6 Ostava are a Bulgarian alternative rock band and "Stop" is a song from their third album, Mono (2004).

The Circle of Life[1]

The dried leaves are beautiful but dead. They rot and turn into food for plants that give birth to new leaves in turn. But these new leaves are different to the old ones. Living matter absorbing the organic energy of dead matter.

Life takes care of the masses, the individual is not a priority. Even if there is a God, He certainly does not respond to one particular person. And neither does God wait on the individual's response.

Human beings experience reincarnation—but as energy, not as personality or consciousness.

What I feel at this very moment, it is the be-all and end-all for me. "After" will never exist.

So am I obliged to be responsible or am I supposed to be a greedy egoist?

If indeed there is no justice after death… Then fear disappears, morality is meaningless and good loses its illusory value. The saints turn into fools and laughing stocks in the eyes of alcoholics like me, drunkards stammering incomprehensibly in the bubbling ditches of life.

A man cannot be of full value to himself during his lifetime. A man disappears after death. In a man there is no sense at all and the circle of life is even more greedy than our selves.

Fear or happiness…

Parenting or impulse…

Primitive stupidity or vain self-destruction…

---

[1] "The Circle of Life" is a fragment from Plamen's first novel, Параноя (*Paranoia*) (Varna: LiterNet, 2007).

St Valentine's Day? Fuck It![1]

I am maundering along the main pedestrian street in Plovdiv, choking under its February dirt. The kitsch is horrible: flocks of pink, heart-shaped balloons hover over enterprising gypsies; the grubby corpses of plush creatures fall out of another go-getting peddler's sack, rolling along the muddy avenue; and next door to the art galleries of one of the European capitals of culture[2] there runs a tireless trade in slobbery valentine cards made in China and printed with English messages. In front of the theater, the fanatical crowd doesn't even cast a glance at the posters for the next performance. Instead, the people cluster around a rusty stall, caught up in a fight for the last genetically raped, thorn-free roses. Despite the winter cold, the perfumeries leave their doors wide open, letting the owners experience their annual orgasm. Queues of eager, glossy, militant "lovers" besiege Plovdiv's pubs, pizzerias and bars in an attempt to reserve a front-row place for the coming bacchanalia. An orgy in which one will be beaten, another become pregnant, a third catch an awkward disease, and *all* get drunk and high together in honor of St Valentine. Wretched *chalga* accompanies all these scenes, its clichéd rhythms and vulgar emotions flying over the Turkish paving stones, spreading out from the music shops like the smell of carrion on a hot summer's day.

Chalga is not love! It is just another repulsive form of commercial kitsch! St Valentine is not the idol of love, but the god of manipulative manufacturers who have sunk their teeth firmly into the degraded flesh of human emotion.

I leave. I have managed to endure the crowd long enough to obtain two bottles of full-bodied red wine, a packet of spaghetti and some aromatic joss sticks. I am home. First, to set the playlist for tonight. Next, place the spaghetti on the hotplate and sample the wine just to make sure that its flavor complements Nirvana's "Come As You Are," Pearl Jam's "Black," Radiohead's "All I Need," P.I.F.'s "Song" and Ostava's "Lonely Man."[3] When everything is ready I turn off the lamps and wait for her to come, comfortably sheltered in the snug of the aromatic wax flames.

But she does not know about me…

The love within us cannot be bequeathed. A man loves only for himself. You love because you need to love, flying in beatific spaces because you desire to fly; suffering because you want to suffer. But there is no one before you. The person in love finds only a dream, a notion, an ideal. You fall in love with nothing but your own dreams—the only carriers of your true longings. Sometimes you manage to personify your dreams in another. Sometimes it's not a single-player game. This doesn't make love any less primal or selfish. I am sure, however, that it makes it quite different and infinitely more real than the love portrayed by the smell of Chinese plush and the soundtrack of *chalga*'s soft-porn music!

---

[1] First conceived for the Plovdiv lifestyle magazine *Mylife*, "Şt Valentine's Day? Fuck It!" was then built into Plamen's second novel, *Имаго* (*Imago*) (Smashwords, 2012).

[2] Plovdiv is one of Bulgaria's candidate cities for the European Capital of Culture in 2019.

[3] "Come As You Are" is from Nirvana's album *Nevermind* (1991); "Black" is from Pearl Jam's album *Ten* (1991); "All I Need" is from Radiohead's album *In Rainbows* (2007); "Song" is from P.I.F.'s album *P.I.F.* (2000); and "Lonely Man" is from Ostava's album *After Love in the Time of War* (2002).

The true fading colours of an illusory love . . . .

Censorship[1]

We are primitive beings with censored lives.

Our genes are the primary carriers of our existential restrictions. Healthy or sick; beautiful or ugly; slim or fat; talented or talentless; brave or cowardly… Genetics determine whether we get fuck-all or whether we fuck; whether the doors of the party are opened to us or closed in our faces. Enormous efforts of self-improvement are of no great import—expending such energy shifting the weights of the status quo out of balance is just not worth it in the long term. For everyone has a destiny. A destiny not found in the pages of a hefty book; a destiny not found in heaven or in hell. No, our destinies are embedded in our bodies.

The first tools of censorship are our parents. They teach us what to eat, when to bathe, when to sleep, when to laugh, and when to cry. They determine whether we are Bulgarians or Macedonians, Christians or Muslims, Communists or Fascists. Mom and dad distinguish bad from good, weird from normal, and scary from useful. They take a primitive human nature and clothe it in social adequacy. They stitch their kids up in it. This uniform coalesces with the human body to such an extent that we cannot feel it. And, over the years, most of us never take this costume off, not even to wash or to patch it. Throughout our lives we hide emotions and impulses in the deep pockets of this garment, embarrassed by the nakedness of our minds. Like any clothing, it grows too small for us, it goes out of fashion and stops suiting us. But our parents will always like it—not because they dressed us in it but rather because, in their eyes, we remain kids forever.

The next red mark of the censor's pen differentiates reality from appearance. Do not underestimate the difference between reality and appearance! From the first moment a child looks at an overbearing TV screen (or computer monitor) until the end of his life, he will seek out images that teach him how to get pleasure. The differences between reality and appearance define our concepts of "losers" and "leaders;" "cool" and "shit;" "success" and "failure." These differences indicate to us what we should strive for and what we must shun at any price. The media tells us what a good life is and how we can buy it. It explains to us what love is and who is not worthy of it.

Then we find a job. The job censors our freedom, putting it into a schedule, consuming it with workdays, leaving us to chew its cud on the weekend.

So here we are today—blind, deaf and dumb slaves, the lowest common multiples of primitive instincts, musty educations and a vicious media reality. And our time is running out, and its trail will stop when the glitter of Death's scythe censors our very existence.

---

[1] "Censorship" is a fragment that has only previously appeared in *Paranoia* (Smashwords, 2012), the English translation of Plamen's first novel, Параноя (Varna: LiterNet, 2007).

Good Morning[1]

I open my eyes sharply, emerging into myself. Startled and confused, breathing hot air in panic. Parched throat seared by constrained cough. Hands holding creased, sweaty sheets tight. I am trembling faintly. This is quite normal, I am used to waking up like this—suffocated by the darkness of dreams that press every fragment of my inadequate consciousness in the moment before my brain fully awakes. At first I thought that these were nightmares, able to squeeze through gaps of incomprehension to stalk behind tightly closed eyelids... There was a time when I placed a notebook and pen by the bed.

The visions of sleep are most vivid just at the point of awakening. You can still catch their fiery threads, slip and slide on them; scroll back your existence in your own puzzling consciousness. With a pen and a notebook by your bed, you can describe this second life every morning. And I was describing it. I guess my passion was driven by a strong love of life. I didn't want to lose the slightest moment of existence, not even the unreal moments.

I enjoyed my strange hobby but failed to pay attention to the burning tension in my neck caused by my brain's straining to remember. I no longer keep a notebook by the bed. It is senseless. My dreams are melted and gone. The aspiration to describe them rationally banished them. I don't dream. When I am asleep there is only darkness. Heavy darkness, the crushing blackness of nothingness, suffocating me with its clinical absence. Sometimes I think that nothing has color and all is dry black.

Sunbeams break like waves as the wind toys with the azure curtains. The breeze slips through the half-opened window bringing the calm hubbub of Plovdiv. The engine rumble, the voices of the people, the birds that welcome spring with their song—a hubbub so relaxing in its infinity. I am stretching slowly, staring at the ceiling. In my mind there are fading, meaningless shadows. I rise and sit up in bed with folded arms.

I enter the bathroom but leave the light off. The twinkle of the burning electricity would cut my sleepy nerves like a razor blade cutting into a fillet of fresh dead fish. I leave the door ajar so I can enjoy the pale daylight creeping in from my bedroom. The bathroom is humid and muggy. I stretch out my arms and freeze. Sweat droplets erupt on the surface of my skin. They mix with each other as if they are alive, forming streams that glide over the sensitive receptors of the epidermis, tickling maddeningly. The shower is broken again. Chlorinated drops break off the spout, sweep silently into the darkness and splosh upon the wet floor. The asymmetric water shrapnel sprays my feet. I turn on the cold water. The jet spills over my body which is still maundering in the nothingness of sleep. The blast of water cripples my hot brain, tightens my chest and refreshes me with pain. I turn on the warm water, adjusting the temperature to enjoy the pleasant cool waves that fill my ears, nose, eyes and throat. It is dark. The cool twilight of the bathroom is different from the clinical darkness of nothingness that I am so afraid of. I cast down my head with open eyes, waiting for the water to drain. I can make out the wet smoke; the steam winding through the half-opened door. Microscopic splashes climb the pale light to merge with thin air and disappear forever in the cycle of everything. I turn off the water and take the soap in my hand. I spend it slowly over my body, enjoying its scent in the darkness. This is not a habit but a ritual. Every morning my entity is refreshed, plucked from nowhere and thrown into the morning of reality. Like the water vapor, I disappear each night to reappear each morning, just the same and yet another.

And yet the same…

I sink into the dark corridor, standing naked in front of the old armoire's large mirror. Gaping my big green eyes, waiting to see who will cast down his head first—my reflection or I. I am not so stupid nor so crazy. I know who will be first. The foolish game livens me. My mouth stretches into a light ironic smile. I remove an errant strand of hair from my forehead with my hand. I freeze like this for some time, slowly sinking into my own pupils. My eyes can be so distant. The tar darkness sucks in my paralyzed being. The face becomes gray. The vague ironic smile is gone and the lips lose their color, fading to bleak ash. Darkness has replied to my eyes. The absolute darkness that lurks deep within my pupils wants me. The adrenaline is bubbling in my muscles, but instincts cannot break away from the hypnosis of my own mind. The hands tremble. Droplets of burning sweat are irrigating the forehead. I must focus on something other than the darkness if I want to tear myself out and throw myself back into reality. I will succeed. This is not a serious crisis—merely a morning greeting from the madness. I just have to grasp the colors. It's easy. My iris—a crystalline green treacle with pale beige and brown graffiti and shining blue sparks at the bottom. These sparks flash like flares, heating and melting the brown, the beige and the green. A mandala of colors with perfect proportions that no man can draw—an explosion of life that will cause my eye muscles to shrink the black pupil. I wink and close my eyes, breathing. I resurface. I am the first to cast down my head, leaning my forehead on the mirror. I am smiling again—not ironically or with relief, but crazily. I look again. There behind the sweaty wet mark of my skin is me. The reflection hides its selfish triumph, but I feel its unhealthy joy.

Hmm. Good morning yourself.

---

[1] "Good Morning" is an extract from Plamen's first novel, *Параноя* (*Paranoia*) (Varna: LiterNet, 2007).

A Spiritual Blast[1]

They say it's New Year's Eve... But why? At first there was the Big Bang and now our universe hosts the after party which continues to pulse to beats and rhythms that dictate the very location of the earth. We know that our planet describes its orbit round the sun in 365.2564 days, but we do not know the exact starting point. That is why every moment, every single second the earth is completing a lap around its star—at least it seems like that if you compare our current position to the one 365.2564 days ago. Then there is the theory of matter's continuous expansion which basically states that, in spite of all their liposuctions, the bodies of the *chalga* stars (prematurely aged through vanity and sexual amortization) continue to grow by thousands of miles in space. Of course they can't detect this growth, despite spending hours in front of the mirror wondering which clothes and cosmetics will best conceal the furrows of cellulite that expose their faded butts. Matter increases proportionally, you know. The proof of this theory can be found in men's rounded wine-skin stomachs. It also means that New Year's Eve does not exist because the earth, rushing across the matter of time, striving to its end, never crosses the same location in space. And if there is no New Year, there is no end to the fiscal year and no taxes—so there is more for beer, vodka, synthetic experiments and all kinds of porn. Right now I am surrounded by all these goods, the masterpieces, the magnificent achievements of millions and billions of years of evolution of certain proteins due to some sort of radiation. But the only thing I care about is that New Year's Eve is a fucking illusion, an absolute lie—an abstract concept people have created to watch over their own lives which are constantly slipping out of control.

I can dimly hear a digitally degenerated voice counting down with heavy timbre.

—5, 4, 3, 2, 1…

Here comes my favorite moment. The lights fade, the music subsides, and the madness of those intolerant of their own emotions and vocal chords melts into the darkness of the crowd. This takes only half a second… but thanks to the shock my head received when I fell from a pear tree in my village as a kid; or perhaps due to the chemical compounds that my heart shoots through my boiling and gurgling blood (spirit bullets affecting the nerves, diverting the brain to blow up the mind)—thanks to these, or this, or something, I have the gift to slow the time around me. Maybe I can stop that sense of matter increasing proportionally; maybe I can manage to escape from the prison of these dimensions and distinguish the matter of time from the matter of existence. Like a sunbeam obstructed by a hand.

Now, just before digital chaos explodes in columns with hundreds of lasers and spotlights, just a few seconds before the people start to roar eagerly and with a freedom from anxiety (because they have a reason to be primitive), at that very moment I feel how the earth takes a deep breath. I feel the warmth of the thousands of bodies around me—the insane who have chosen to shelter their minds at this house party in the winter night. I hear the falling of every graceful snowflake outside before the drifts swallow up the individuality. I have enough time to fly. I can go up to the mountains, slip into a dark den, curl up on the wet moss next to the huge and hairy torso of a hibernating bear and watch the animal's powerful lungs exhale white steam until I dissolve myself and touch the stars. We can do all of that in just a second! We have all the time in the world, but we are unable to spend it because we only know how to obey the physical matter about us.

—HAPPY NEW YEAR! BOOM! And BOOM! And BOOM! And BOOM! And BOOM!

Then savage shouts, a twisted outpouring of human passion, screams that tear the universal harmony. Bright light blasts my eyes. I no longer need my active consciousness. It is time for it to sleep, to rest. My head recoils from an explosive wave wiping out the hall. My body stutters in an attempt to read the message from the digital genius behind the DJ's console. This murderer of my moments of timelessness, this prophet of ephemera, this fake Buddha! Some people wave hands and honor his great-ness; others embrace each other, inspired by a samaritan love engendered through digital and synthetic substances; and then there are those who just drink to celebrate the moment—the moment when everyone truly yearns for an illusory new be-ginning. No—I don't need my active consciousness. It dreams, dreams of music, sings "Who Am I" in its sleep,[2] roaming with that phlegmatic super rumble of frank sadness, that absolute personification of human helplessness. Arms move as though disconnected, head tilts, and feet stagger willfully. My body shakes with fiery rage in this innate pseudo-dance, but even behind tightly closed eyelids I can still see the crooked shadows of the others existing near me. My autopilot suggests to them that I am feeling absolute pleasure, thoroughly soaked with liquor, but my mind is no longer here—it is silently dreaming non-existent memories of happier reveries.

[1] Part of "A Spiritual Blast" appeared in the Plovdiv magazine *Mylife*, it was then built into *Paranoia* (Smashwords, 2012), the English translation of Plamen's first novel, *Параноя* (Varna: LiterNet, 2007).

[2] "Who Am I" is a song from Peace Orchestra's first album, *Peace Orchestra* (1999).

Synthetic Timelessness[1]

I am by the window, wrapped in the cozy warmth of my home, watching the winter outside. Plovdiv is a southern town. It snows rarely. And, when it does, the fine white crystals are brutally repressed by the censorship of global warming. Even if some snowflakes make it through, they are usually tatty and gray and almost immediately turn into muddy and sticky slush. The winter beneath the hills is not like the fairy-ice whiteness that wraps Belegast in Bogdan Rusev's tales.[2] It is more like the scruffy frosted canvas used by my neighbor to cover his Lada.[3]

Today, however, it is cold…

The TV is vomiting out the national media's morning broadcast. Some fat gentleman, dressed in shabby gray and ugly brown, is furiously explaining the harm of drugs. His huge jelly cheeks quake with the rumble of a nicotine cough. The skin beneath his eyes resembles calluses full of alcohol. This gentleman is a psychologist and is evidently quite knowledgeable. He is foaming with rage and erudition, expounding that marijuana causes schizophrenia, that cocaine causes strokes, and that amphetamines doom their users to heart attacks. The guy reduces the various drugs to the common denominators of psychosis. He points an accusing finger at the poor standards of living in Bulgaria, standards that attack the family unit, destroy ideals and unleash various forms of dependence. The gentleman defends his thesis brilliantly and with a great sense of satisfaction. Then he sets off for a glass of *rakia* at the nearest tavern, his yellowish fingers crumpling a pack of cigarettes with feverish haste.

I must admit—the psychologist is, indisputably, right.

So fucking what?

Late at night when the heavy red wine rinses away the daily stresses and the burning cigarette ends provide an illusory feeling of coziness, it is all too easy and natural to deny those others, those zombies sunk in the white timelessness of the trenches and the ruins. Most people are dependent on legal drugs but this is somehow not an obstacle to seeing an enemy in every underground addict. Our society cannot wait for the next outcry over excise on *rakia*.[4] Then, to show that they have an active civic position, the true Bulgarian will also bandy slogans against the junkies and the gypsies. "Build a camp!"—they say—"Build it on a remote island on the Danube and shut them up there! This is how our society will help, this is how we will cure the infection... and let's run a current through the barbed wire!"[5]

Dependence on drugs is not a disease, it is not a virus, it is not something that stalks only the dregs of society. Drug addiction is REALIZED EMOTIONAL DEFICIENCY SYNDROME.[6] The addict does not hunt after psychological euphoria, does not pursue a surge of vital energy, does not seek a chemical frenzy to create crimes. No, usually the dependent just wants to crawl out from underneath the impersonal society of the normals, seeking shelter from the hypocritical mask of the quotidian. The junkie ignites his feelings with ugly synthetic substances, and the emotions that were meant to last for a lifetime burn away in full force in a couple of short years.

The dependence on drugs is not an economic problem. It is determined by the horrific emotional recession silting up human societies everywhere. The addictions are derived from an emotional bankruptcy peculiar to our arrogant civilization. The blame lies with every single person. The responsibility, however, is assumed by those with the most emotional natures.

I am still by the window, wrapped in the cozy warmth of my home, watching the winter. It is cold… Somewhere along the dirty ditches of life, lurking on the slopes of the hills, hiding in the ruins of the town, there are the children of a whole lost generation. They have sunk their souls in the white timelessness of drugs, wandering about in memories of impossible emotions. And I wonder—do I really care about them and their forgotten fiery visions? Do I take pity on those redeeming everyone's guilt…

---

[1] "Synthetic Timelessness" is extracted from Plamen's second novel, *Имаго* (*Imago*) (Smashwords, 2012).

[2] Bogdan Rusev is a contemporary Bulgarian writer and lifestyle journalist. Belegast is a legendary city from his books.

[3] The Lada 1300 was the most common automobile in Bulgaria during the late communist period—there are still many working models on the streets today.

[4] *Rakia* is a strong alcoholic drink popular in Bulgaria. After public pressure, the Bulgarian government tried to secure from the EU a reduction in excise costs for *rakia*.

[5] There was a communist concentration camp in Bulgaria on the island of Belene in the river Danube.

[6] *Emotional Deficiency Syndrome* is the name of Plamen's literary series (still unpublished in its entirety) containing the novels *Imago* and *Paranoia*.

Devon Pearse & James Wilson
divertissements

Hello

A two-sentence email: "They're tearing down the old house. See you there Thursday at 4." Three years of silence suddenly ended. Of course she showed. Implied urgency woke undead curiosity. And there are ties that can't be severed. Not with time. Nor distance. Not even with ignorance or knowledge. They reach inside and beyond all that, like the rhizomes and root systems of certain aggressive plants. Cut them, prune them. Clear away the top surface. Burn it to the ground. But they are still there: underneath and always. A festering, spreading influence, unseen and impossible to remove. Impractical to rationalize how they ever got planted in the first place. The notice for demolition was fixed to the front gate. Almost as terse as his email. She gave the latticed ironwork a tap with her shoe, the kind of cautious touch it had never received from her before. The prodding of a corpse. It opened. Check phone again. Expect to see a message of non-explanatory excuse. But nothing. She went into the front garden. Full of split blue sacks of cement. A rusting upturned bathtub leant against the living room window sill. Its back to the world. Shamed and cowering. A final attempt to preserve its flaking dignity from the public glare. *Living room*. She almost laughed. The windows and door were boarded up. The house looked like a stitched-up cadaver after all of its organs had been removed. Some taxidermist's plaything. The hair and nails of a corpse continue to "grow" after death and this body was no exception. Buddleia had pushed through the slabs of the pathway. Ragwort and wallflowers broke through on the roof where, in places, so many tiles had fallen down that some of the bare timber beams could be seen. Unnerving. Like seeing the bone through a deep clean cut. She walked round the front of the house circumspectly, a visitor to a gallery where she found her own memories on display in a hideously distorted form. She stopped. The fire escape they had climbed barefoot in the summers to feel the cool of the metal that was always trapped in the alley's shade. Up to the balcony and the sunshine. The plastic chairs and the parasol. She touched the railing, scared or hopeful that it would all come tumbling down, dissolve into another time. "It's not safe" someone uttered behind her. "No. It's probably not," she said, turning around to face the past that could not be demolished.

Hello

Gray skies. Darkening her soul. Waiting for the bell. The sound that breaks the clouds. For another afternoon that turns to evening and to night and then to sleep so it can all begin again, shaken free, awakened by another bell.

Alone in the car, she watches the rain. She sees them play through her breath upon the window. The only way she knows that she's alive. An image through the mist. The thoughts of all that she's forgotten and let go. Waiting. Always waiting. Never going anywhere. Trying not to notice, not to recognize the truth. Drown out all the voices in her head, in the car, questions drifting through the house and up the stairs, finding her. "Leave me alone!" she wants to scream. "Why can't you ever let me be? Let me believe—let me be me." There's nowhere left to hide. Nowhere she can breathe. No one she can talk to—just her own voice deep inside. A whisper no one else would ever hear, resounding with the loneliest reply.

"Hello?"

Force another smile. Forcing down the fear that if she stops to wonder, stops believing in the lie, she'll disappear. Hide the things she won't allow herself to tell them. Quell the desire to create, within a dream, a reality that only she can know. Something, only one, that's all her own. One thing that no one else can handle or destroy. Can't leave their fingerprints on for her to wipe away. There are things that she's forgotten, set aside and left to dream. One day she plans to return for them. The captive one inside her calls her back. "I can't wake up, I can't get out!" Pleading with her, tearing her apart. Everyone will have their say. Tell her what she should and has to do. Huddled in a corner of the room, holding on to curtains, fingers clutching at the rug. Arms wrapped tight about her knees. A slamming door downstairs. The sound of laughter, little feet upon the floorboards. Her own voice hollow in the stillness of another afternoon, "I'll handle things. We'll make it one more day. Don't cry."

Too early, wide awake. Wide open eyes. The wind like breath upon her doorstep. Memories of a white dress. Of flowers with dried petals like the years with all the beauty gone. The tears, the joy. The waiting for the feeling that it all meant something more. Siphoned youth and photographs to remind her of the one she was expected to become. While they sleep, she tiptoes through the house. Afraid. Alive. "You have to breathe. Only you know how much I deserve to live. Remember. I'm still here."

Snow falling, with a coat to keep her warm. Driving slowly down the road. Not looking back. A note left on the table. "I'm sorry. I couldn't help but wake."

Fade Into You

*T*he air—the thought that you could steal my breath and
give it back with all of you inside. Stay here with me. I want
to see you. Please, give me your hand. Just let me in.

The way your gaze would hold me close, seeing you see me.
All I'd ever wanted—to look into the eyes of someone else
and find myself. Take my hand. Forget to breathe. A blank slate.
A clean canvas. No preconceived ideas of who I am or who
you thought I'd be. A mirror with no blemishes, no cracks
to let the lies seep through. A wish to see my everything in
nothing. Palm to palm, our fingers interlaced. A shattering
sound like bells, like the breaking of a shell. A breaking into
truth. And suddenly I'd see me there, pouring out of your eyes,
out of your soul and finally, effortlessly, the pieces that were
left would fall away. Fade together into me. The me inside your
eyes. Becoming real. Breathing in the truth.

Please, just don't look back. You'll fall apart...

I wanted so to be the same for you—the reflection no one
else could ever see. Turning on the light, I wondered why you
fled from it; a shadow fast escaping, leaping past me into black.
I told myself I shouldn't be afraid. It was a different truth I
feared; I only needed you to see it. But the image wasn't real
enough to you. How sad, when all you ever had to do was just
believe. Now belief is fading. Fading into you. Darkening your

eyes, clouding the reflection. All the colors gone. As if they, perhaps, were never really there.

Strange... you never knew.

Fading. Away from me. Walking backwards. Back into yourself, a part of everything you feared. How could you go? Everything is broken. Each fragment is another jagged memory. Reflected beauty, mirrored pain. Can't stand to look, can't bear to pick them up. Remember what you can't escape. Let it follow you and force your heart to dance. Let it turn upon itself. Pain to beauty, past to present, love to hate. Forget to breathe. Forget to fear the truth.

You left me in the darkness. So much silence. Pieces falling. Alone in all the fragments of myself. A broken soul—a heart without a shelter. And then a light—a voice from far away. A stranger who had captured all my tears, collected them and made of them a pool. I look inside and see myself. I smile as I start to disappear. "You're fading into you," he says, echoing my thoughts. Alone. Complete. The product of the dust you left behind. Still wondering where I've come from. "You've been here all along," he tells me.

"Strange... you never knew."

Fade Into You

You kept on cutting out. I couldn't hear you properly. It wasn't that I didn't want to know. Oh, how I wanted to know! But you kept yourself hidden. Remained a fading voice. And I only heard my own words in you. I didn't mean to get frustrated. I didn't mean to frustrate. The tail-ends of your sentences trailing into tremulations unseen. I think I'd like them back. But you punish me with stony silence. And an absence so unsure. And then I thought I began to see you everywhere I went. I saw you on the Underground, half a carriage down. Were you wearing my coat? I saw you through a shop window. You walked with my own gait. I saw you on the TV. I hadn't switched it on. I saw you in an elevator. We both had headphones in. These stubborn and uncomfortable silences are revealing more about who we are. I had to get away because these glimpses were driving me wild. And I didn't know what I was glimpsing! I left the glassy city with its artificial illuminations. Found a homestead in the hills. I took a path by moonlight and walked it where it went. My thoughts were errant, absconded with the day. My eyes were keen as the huntsman's, taking in every breeze-blown leaf. Then I heard the sound of water and it reminded me of you. Murmurations. All the words you said that I never quite heard. Too open to interpretation by their fractured forms and evasive volumes, their petered pitch and tacit tones. And the way wound on until it reached the water's edge where I was dumb and truly struck. For there you were, gazing up at me in vacant splendor, projected majesty. We mimic each other's amazement. Stare with the same scrutiny. Cup the silence like ellipses. The skimming wing of a pipistrelle, the other side of the pool, breaks some kind of spell. The lines across your face cause me no small sorrow. Why can't they be gone and just be so? Is it wrong that I think I know you? Is it wrong that I can't avert my eyes? You're not beautiful, but familiar. And I find that enchanting. Like the childlike fascination of lifting up a rock and watching the darkling beetles crawl. Can you make me happy? Is it you that makes me sad? I won't try to hold my breath. But I am going to go under.

So Low, So High

The world's a spiral. My heart's a spiral too. Mr Fibonacci, my sights are trained on you. Scattered flocks and clap of wings. Petals drop and roots dig in. The world is sinking high and I am rising low; we form a helix, a micro-macro to and fro. There is no difference between where I go at night and where I wake up next day. The horror is all mine and the beauty too. Twist the lens and change the slides. Magic lantern eyes and kaleidoscopic minds. It's only natural that my frustrations escape in the inarticulate violence of others; that my thoughts manifest themselves in looted shops, burnt-out buses, and smoldering police cars. That my feelings are caught on CCTV veiled in makeshift bandannas, concealed under sportswear cowls, throwing paving stones and Molotov cocktails at notional authorities. Take the bottle. And light it. The bottle's a symbol. A vehicle of intense explosion and devastation. The world's a spiral. My heart's a spiral too. So scratch around the floor with a dalit's dignity and pick up the shards and melt them down and cast them and... get someone to punch through the facade. It's only sugar glass. Won't graze your knuckles. Might soothe your beating heart. I built a twenty-first-century folly to match my own design. It took me years. I trapped myself inside. I sanded and polished each brick to make them smooth as... glass. And I mooned around in circles like a goldfish going nowhere... fast. Safety and comfort lost syllables. Safe and fort. The circles trapped me in a two-dimensional plane. When I finally looked up and down, I almost went insane. So I got out my grappling hooks, my crampons, even found an *echelier*. Didn't think in French. Just thought and one day it was there. My feet broke the rungs. I wore the ropes so thin. I climbed and fell a countless lot but wasn't giving in. My folly was a well shaft. My folly was a cell. But now that I can spiral I can leave this see-through hell. Outside things are in ruins, so I smash my folly down. Let it join the rubble of this razed and run-down part of town. This is not annihilation. Everything will be recycled. If we're unlucky, we'll build up everything the same as it was before. But the variables are vast. I am not the only one who feels well rid of walls—all about people are rolling up their sleeves, pushing back their hoods and feeling the sun's rays upon their skin. The rays were never absent, we just had to let them in. The world's a spiral. My heart's a spiral too. I will destroy it. I will rebuild it too.

So Low, So High

A shadow falls across the sandcastle. The cherubic youth squints into the sun, shielding his eyes with a frown and the back of his hand. She kicks the tallest turret down, then giggles as she runs away. Did he bother to rebuild it? I've often wondered through the years, and wondered if I wondered as I ran that day. Sand so warm, burning the arches of my feet, setting my soles on fire. I never looked back. Playing hide and seek with the wind in my kingdom made of dunes. I don't recall that I felt sorry for it, this destruction I'd impelled. It seemed the very art of inspiration; my own gift to him. And it was crooked, anyway.

Sometimes I think I lost myself somewhere within those dunes; a natural progression, a forgetting of the things that make us who we are. Our childhood runs away, leaving us to linger in its wake. The inescapable exchange; the mourning and the joy. So acceptable. So necessary. All so we can grow up, but at what cost? We build our towers so that in the end, when we stand amongst the rubble of the days we've left behind we can say that we'd give anything to have it back. Brand new and glistening, like the morning on the waves. We're captured in the rise and fall. I want to feel it all again.

And so I thought one day I'd give it up—banish this perception of the here and now and what. Never too late. Never truly forgotten. Warm sand on the boardwalk. I let my sandals dangle from my fingers, barely hanging on, so aloof, so carefree. I think

I'll get a sunburn just to feel. The air can make you weightless, lift you up like a balloon, or like a kite that dances high, still reaching for the clouds but tethered to a child's tight-closed hand. Hold on, I think. Remember how it feels, even when it makes you want to cry.

I close my eyes, then open them again—the world gone white and pale all around. An old man sits upon the sand, gazing at the sea and his own relinquished memories. My shadow falls across his thoughts. "I remember you," he says. "You kicked down my sandcastle!"

Quiet Place

A nother morning brings the sunrise and I'm chasing my own shadow. Down an alleyway, across the street, walking somewhere I could swear I've never been. I could swear I am alive.

Children dancing round a maypole, colors twisting, fused together, apart, together again. Tangling, untangling, making their own way. Around and round. Around and round and round once more. Braiding together, bleeding together, like ballerinas waltzing with besotted marionettes. I watch them spin beneath the restless clouds. The shifting days, the falling leaves that mingle with the ribbons in their hair.

Some minutes later and I pull myself away. Too much unity can make you long for freedom. It's like falling through a rainbow, a reflection on a pane, ripples in a puddle flowing outwards from the center of it all. Till there is no breath to catch. Has it all been done before? Am I asleep upon lush grass in a pool of golden sunlight? Does my shadow lie beneath me as my mind escapes in search of quietude?

On fragile, beating wings I'm lifted, up and over every garden wall. Summer roses kissed with dewdrops, silken fortresses abandoned by their skilled and ardent weavers. The creation done, they free-fall, linked only by a thin, translucent thread. How meticulous, how free this life can be. A wish upon a whisper; a cloud blown by the wind.

There are shadows by the river cast by trees that touch the sky. At night I think they fall into the water to be carried out to sea, gathered up by waves and flung upon another shore. A Gypsy woman waits for them; she walks along the sand collecting shades of other times, and all the stars upon the ocean and the shells beneath her feet. Her dark eyes smile and yet are laced with sorrow. Too much to know; too much I cannot tell.

A cottage with lace curtains; a robin's egg; the sound of chimes like church bells far away. Wet pavement colored by the city lights, dark and bright while all the world lies sleeping. When will it be time to live again? Or do we live while yet we dwell in dreams?

Quiet Place

Y ou absorb it through your soles. Cracked heels, calluses and blisters are signs of knowledge. Call me peripatetic. I say autodidact. I am never walking away. I am always walking to. My journey is a perpetual return. Yet all I see is new. Dawn precipitation upon a spider's web. So much weight strung on such a slender thread. There are lessons to be learnt from every patch of ground. That's why I changed my name to Naïf the Wonderclown. I didn't paint my face. I just discarded a mask. And I could see so much better. I used to dream of retiring to some cave of my own where I would hear my heart boom like a bittern, echo round and round, reverberate until it reached the all-encompassing om, deafening every need and thought and I would disappear, as swiftly and suddenly as someone pulling shut the slats on a venetian blind. But, as Naïf, I realized that I didn't have to fade out, I could fade in—walk everywhere, soak it all up, and *become* everywhere. This was not desertion by a disenfranchised nabob, a middle-ranking misanthrope's make-do, nor some penny-lacking poet's purdah to screen away the world. No. My silence, my observation, my persistent pacing of this planet's face were not marks of difference or aloofness, but an embrace of existence, funneling every aspect through my ever-curious feet. I clocked the culmination when I took cover under a bandstand in a park and listened to the breaking rain on the tin roof. My continual return was over: I had been here before as a child. To go on would be to retrace covered ground. To go back would be the same. So I sat and listened to the static crackle of the rain. The rat-a-tat-tat of its knuckles' rap duly dimmed and died away. The sun nudged apart the clouds and the eternal photons fractured me into variegated hues that arced in all directions. Futureproofed and past-protected. Now. I am.

Floating

I am a doorkeeper. I do not bar the way. Quite the opposite. I'm more of an observer, an onlooker. I would love to welcome everyone in, but that is not permitted. Neither can I reject people. That too is not permitted. I make sure the door is always open. Clear of external obstacles and supercilious distractions. Everyone must look through. And then they choose. Sometimes people hover on the threshold. Sometimes they ask questions, most of which I am unable to answer. Sometimes their interrogations take a more personal line. They might ask whether I once went through the door (to which the answer is "Yes"), or they might ask why I went through the door (to which I have been unable to formulate a proper answer). Sometimes they ask me what it was like, this moment of entrance that they must contemplate. Once, against my better judgment, I attempted an answer. I could only answer in the present tense, for the feeling has never really left me. "The warmth wells up," I said, "I am melting away, but becoming the surest, most solid I have ever been. I cannot move how I used to. I follow my eyes, but my eyes are not my eyes, they are… me! I am being drained away, but not diminished. I am being subsumed by others yet gaining identity. I am with her." And they said, quite angrily, "But it doesn't feel like that for us at all." And I realized then that it was different for everyone. And that made me feel a sadness that I hadn't felt before. But I eventually came to terms with this sadness and, unnoticed, it morphed into a gratitude. A gratitude for all the infinite diversity of feeling, the variety of experience. All that I had not known. All that I could never know. But I did intuit that all of this, all of this, came from a single source. And that was enough for me to feel that I had shared in everything.

Floating

My indifference is pervasive. Regret festooned upon my soul, I'm moving away from something. Trying not to want. Hoping not to need. I suffer from an inequality of virtue to necessity. It's just too much to ask for. And all roads lead to somewhat the same desinence. I come here to remind myself of that.

"I never really loved your grandmother," he says to me in a voice rich with candor once mistaken for remorse. I lack the heart to remind him we're not related. A few penitent hours a week, I sit with him in his threadbare room, surrounded by the accumulations of long life. Getting longer, never fuller. Eyes becoming dull, seeing yesterdays through a veil of hazy years. Memories are sweeter than life. He keeps a box beside his bed, filled with his exiguous possessions. When he grasps hold of one filament of thought that leads him down some long forgotten road, he sometimes rifles through the contents, lifting out a trinket, holding up a photograph, dog-eared and faded, fashioned in an old-time style.

Today he dislodges an old playbill, along with a fluttering of dust and dry, colorless rose petals, and extends his arm in my direction, the creased talisman clutched between trembling fingers. "What is it?" I inquire. With the index finger of his other hand, he stabs at the playbill, fiercely indicating the photograph on the cover. I take the antiqued pages from him, making a show of reverence I don't yet apprehend.

My eyes behold a dancer, frozen in a graceful affectation, one arm outstretched, hand reaching into nothingness, gaze fixed on perpetuity. "Genevieve," he breathes, as though the name conveys her soul. As his story is begun, relived within the telling, I feel myself drift back with him. I see him in his younger days as he stands outside the theater, shoes polished, hair slicked neatly into place. He brings with him the roses, the bouquet of his affections, symbolically displayed but not yet gifted. They are pale, lovely blossoms, their delicate petals figurantes in an efflorescent whorl.

He mingles with the crowd, taking his seat within the audience, one more face amongst the crowd. He watches as she floats on air. Each pirouette can stop his breath. He would die to dance with her, to hold her in his arms. A swirling, rising, aching pitch. The swell of melody; the falling of the curtain. One final bow and she is gone.

Last to leave, he follows the crowd into the street. Alone, he waits outside the door. Always waiting. Never doing. He hears her footfalls and her laughter. She is seldom lonely. With pounding heart, once more betrayed by loathsome cowardice, he sets the flowers on the ground, making his escape around the corner.

She steps out into the street, company and glee all but forgotten. Looking all about, so nearly lost, she retrieves the flowers, drawing them close, inhaling the sweet fragrance of unspoken admiration. Unnoticed on the sidewalk, she waltzes with the roses, as around the corner he stands and watches, clutching a single petal. A token of remembrance for another wasted chance.

"I was a fool," he says, and I dolefully agree as he relates how she took ill one summer having just returned from... where was it now? Paris? London? Some other far-off place where her floating feet had hypnotized the masses. Perhaps had made them feel the way he had. Perhaps had made them fall in love. So many fools.

She was buried in a nearby town and never was her grave in want of roses.

His words trail off, his hand slips to his side and he sleeps. I am shaken by the thoughts my visit has evoked. I wander through the streets, opining wordlessly of fools and who they love. Of fools grown old.

That night I dream of a dancer, of his Genevieve, and she is floating, floating, just as he described. Into his room, to where he sighs in his sleep. I imagine he awakens as a younger man, bolder than he was in life, and rises, offering his hand. Her fingers slip into his grasp, her eyes alight with recognition of the admirer she never knew in life.

I return the following day to find him, there in his deserted room, content, at peace, no longer of this world. His body rests, surrounded by playbills and petals, these melancholy trifles lending an eloquent ambiance of hope to an otherwise sorrowful repose. The denouement of a life led by a solitary fool. Upon his lips he wears the remnant of a smile.

Perhaps not so alone. Perhaps a fool no more.

Floating

It is at night, after the lights in the laboratories have been turned off, and the technicians and scientists have gone home, that they start to sing. And they don't just sing. They *glow*. All sorts of different colors. Like neon, but… but warmer, more *human*. It's quite a spectacle. The lights flood out the wire-meshed windows and into the corridors. They pour over the polished floor and up the spotless walls. And to walk through this… this phosphorescence. Well, it feels like being bathed in something wonderful. Something wonderful, but also terribly maudlin. For one gets the impression that each light, beautiful though it may be, is just a simulacrum, a projection of something still trapped in the stark and clinical container that houses it. But all this is as to nothing when one hears them sing. They sing the most heart-wrenching songs of yearning. They sing *to each other*, I'm sure. Songs of undying love. Longing to hold hands. And this always chokes me because, as far as I can tell, they are just *voices*. Voices in jars. Shelf after shelf. Vitrine after vitrine of jars. Glass jars empty save for their iridescent lights and ethereal voices. And they sing of touch. They sing of bodies. Sing of desire. And their plaints are so acute and true that I have many times wished to set them free. To smash the jars and give them the release they seem to dream of. To let them fly to each other, lie with each other, commingle in whatever way they can. And I think how I would love to be asleep in bed next to my wife. I don't know how long their song lasts for—I always hear it on a level that makes time seem almost irrelevant. And when I review the CCTV footage at the end of my shift, none of what I have seen or heard is ever recorded. And so I mark in the security log "No incident" and when the technicians and scientists return in the morning, I think to myself: "What mysteries will they never get to see? What mysteries will they fail to experience? What mysteries are they seeking to destroy?" And I drive home and read the note my wife leaves me before she goes to her work.

Asleep From Day

for W.J.A. xxx

Just for today, just for tonight, we regress. Tomorrow: responsibilities, the resumption of problems. But not now. It's been too long since we all just laid back on the grass and watched the clouds creep past in benevolent forms. Watched our shadows move around the dials of our bodies, as the sun turns us into English roses; healthily glowing cherubim. We shall reminisce. Because when we get these rare opportunities, it can sometimes be the only chance we have to ascertain who we are and where we came from. Whether any of it was real. Because sometimes we remember the past no better than the films we have watched or the novels we have more recently read. So we whirl each other's Wurlitzers, spin each other's tops, and go back... Tell the time with dandelions. Illuminate our smiles with buttercups. Salve our wounds with dock leaves. Annunciate the word *cumulonimbus* with faux-RP gravitas. And nudge me. Hide in rhododendrons. Roll sideways down the hill. Garland our hair with laurels. Swim in the chill of the lake. And nudge you. ... If we can't stay there, then let's stay here beneath the sun. Bake me like a stone, destroy me with your rays. I am here to be obliterated. Melt away the hateful words: deadline; overdrawn; commuter. And as the stars come out to play we decide to drop. And we stay and maintain the feeling. We babble about textures and colors, the pools of light from the pavilion lushicizing the grass (is the word we invent). And then we walk out into the darkness beyond, heading to the hedgerows, perhaps subliminally recalling how we used to push the boundaries. (Now we just make them up!) Tonight, though, in our intoxication-induced nostalgia, we stay within the field, just wanting to slip the halogen glow and get a truer color of night. We look round at each other's faces through massively dilated pupils and someone says, "We've got a lot of friends," and the tingle in the belly is stoked, the jelly legs buckle, as we all agree at this amazing and banal realization. And as dawn approaches and we begin to crawl back into our normal selves, dehydrated and dead tired from dancing, you turn and say to me with a strange combination of mischief and innocence, "I can't believe we both ended up with jobs with 'consultant' in their titles!"

Asleep From Day

C olors fly past; your hair whips back into my face as you
pedal down the street, the trees and houses staying
still as they seem to run away. The birds with all their feathers
and the wings that make them fly. I feel them like a heartbeat
that pushes me to soar. I hear the keys upon the piano before
they make a sound. The rushing water and the wind in sharps
and flats and tones that no one else has names for. It is
beautiful and violent and I scream the feeling out and don't
know why.

So many misconceptions. Maybe she was right. Maybe you
should stay away. You've let me stand on my own, and that
feels good. Like a promise—I don't have to be awake inside
your world. I look into your eyes; unspoken secrets like
hushed whispers, the sweetest melancholy. I want to tell you
that I understand—what I've always understood, but cannot
say. I sense your thoughts, take in your sorrow, believe it
almost real to me. I wonder how you see the palette—all
the hues and streams of light and shadow. The iridescent
ramblings of nature, laughter, love. Sometimes real, often
garish, glaring, shouting—telling me to run. I pound my fist
against my head. It makes them turn away because the truth
is seldom gentle. They hide within themselves, they cannot
see me face to face. They are afraid.

But never you. I let you take my hand, and I don't mind, but
you're the only one who can. Others try to talk to me; forced

reluctantly into this ruse by their need to comprehend what frightens them. Like turning on the light to watch the shadows burst. There. Relax now. It was never meant to harm you. Just a curiosity—a boy inside a cage. They each want to be the one to find the explanation. To prove that they can reach me. To pretend to grasp what they could never understand. But you don't try to—you only accept.

You listen to my silence speak and then our own communication can be heard. We watch the stars together, the evening calm surrounding us, drawing forth imagination. The stars, the friends we share; so beautiful. Sparkling eyes look down upon us, so far away, so small. We are insignificant beings with bodies that will one day fade away to reveal the essence of who we really are. The one thing we all share.

And then I'll tell you how I know when you're afraid. How your frustration is complex, although no one would suspect it. It isn't easy like mine; does not explode into cacophony and echo in a garbled sound that was meant to be a word. I'll confess I love your laughter, how it sounds like something falling, like the snow, the rain, the sunlight—all blended into one. I'll bravely talk of how I dream of you, and dream of me, but not me. Me as someone else, someone like you. And I could speak to you with words, real words like others use. I sometimes whisper that I love you, and forget I'm in a dream. You turn to me, your lips touched with a smile, and the daylight fades around you. Forgotten beams of luster illuminate the softness of your hair, your silhouette. Our hands reach out, our fingers almost touch, and then I wake. I am myself again, my own conservator. Entombed within this mottled, changeless shell. Who I am, with nothing to become. Always like I fell asleep within a dream. An endless day still waiting for the night.

We watch the stars together. The stars, the friends we share. Their eyes like yours, so beautiful. So constant in a waking dream. The moonlight. The one thing we all share.

Nightime

Raindrops racing through their brethren on passing car windows. Revolving doors and umbrella-carapaced crowds. The unprepared spat out at the drowned. Their clothes cower closer to their skins, but cannot shy away. Black cabs being hailed in rain-induced rushes by besuited men covering their hair with sodden evening newspapers. Dark at five and the race to get back to the flickering lights of televisions, illuminating the loneliness of so many insides. From buildings backing on to commuter railway lines. Suspended lives. Hanging from straps, afraid of eyes. Or do I project these lies? Unpause the caesura. Stare down the downpour. Plaster my hair across my brow. Apple my cheeks. Adorn my lobes with aqueous bling. I will take it all. My mistakes have been made. I cannot be un-numbed. Pivot on the axle of my hips. Shoulders swivel left and right. As the bolters-home barge me this way and that. I have no hurry. I will soak in this slurry. And dream of absolution. Wet through, I am ignored by the strip lighting in my building's foyer, the elevator doors close without me. I leave puddles on the disinterested stairs. This is semi-fulfilled anonymity. Only half will be the death of me. When the rain abates in the middle of the night, I abandon my ceiling-staring sleeplessness and dress. I am drawn outside. The city is silent and submissive, pliant. Too early for the blackbirds' nocturne. Too late for passers-by. To hear the sound of sturdy-soled shoes slapping the pavement slabs would bring not comfort, but terror. I think I'd prefer terror. To what I have in mind. Invigorated by the spent showers, a slug with a renewed sense of demise, I slide away from these streets that refuse to bear my traces. I pace until the postcodes of the past are fixed on the road signs I have forsaken. Here there is history and meaning in every broken bench, graffitied wall, and shuttered shopfront. I learnt that too late. I arrive in time to see two silhouettes pass the window. There are new curtains, I think. And then the light goes off. I return whence I came, fleeing, foundered, wrecked. "Absolved" for another night. But there is no respite. I reach my building, lean with my back against its indifferent face and slide slowly down to the still damp floor. I need to hurt more.

Nightime

The door swings closed behind me. Immediately I regret my desire to escape—to move again amongst the living. But move I do, forcing my feet forward, guiding my body down the hall and past the stairs, beneath the arch and out into the world. The first thing I notice is the mist, and how the pavement glistens from the rain, the air giving off the pent-up energy of dark, still newly wakened by the night.

I glance reluctantly at strangers as they pass, each caught up in the flow of who they are and who they choose to be. The atmosphere is close, bearing a kinship to the stale breath of buildings, shops and doorways. Nothing fragrant. No aroma here of sodden earth and trees. No freshness to be gained from vacant streets.

It's then I see you there beneath the lamppost, your back pressed against the metal coolness, one knee bent, hands thrust into the pockets of your jeans. The light exhales a halo, encompassing you in a hazy glow—half real, half contrived by an electric shroud of softly diffused brilliance. I pause on the sidewalk, not wanting you to see me yet for fear I'd break this spell, the illusion of this moment so raptured in your solitude, so sure of who you are.

I'm waiting here, not knowing what to say, how to behave, as laughter brushes past me. A sudden crowd sweeps by and then you turn. A sly wind tangles with your hair, leaving it bemused across your forehead.

I draw a breath and then our eyes meet and you smile. And I wish that time could hold us here forever—on a sidewalk, underneath a lamppost, in a misty world of glances from afar.

Something Good

City streets soaked in late autumnal rains; nights pulling in close, tight and asphyxiating. The damp air renders everything a memory. And the present becomes a weeping sore of absence. On another continent the sun laps at your flesh. And I imagine lives we might have had and lives that we might still have and the very notion of possibility renders me useless. You're closer to the desert than I have ever been. But my mind is vast. A scorpion, surrounded by a ring of fire will, sensing the futility, sting itself to death. I remember. I will always remember. It is my curse. No matter how pleasant my experiences I will always be haunted. And now you are my circle of flames. I recall (or do I fantasize?): How we cha-cha-cha'd along the pavements, beneath the lampposts' obsequious bows. Your touch completed my circuit. That's how positive and negative combine. Alternate. Saturate. Consummate. You defied the fondness of absence. My pangs concur, refute. Lizards 'scape your shadow in sun-baked climes. Snails litter my path, tricking me into acts of repossession I have no desire to perform. If we carry our homes on our backs, then the key word is "our," a plural not a singular possessive. I remember. I always remember. I blessed your sneezes. You, the unbeliever, still said "thank you." You typed your feelings on the Qwerty keyboard of my ribs. Now I just long to press "return." If I roll the orbs of my eyes upwards, I can see the same stars as you. You are close to the riddle of the Sphinx; I am pacing circuits beneath the curse of the Shard. You will never know how you answer my questions. I may never know too. But you do. You do. You do. You do.

Something Good

We've looked forward to it for so long, and now the fair has come to town; glittering, mesmerizing, heartbeats racing to the meter of each ride displayed upon the midway. The rise and fall, the dizzy spirals. We'll tackle that one later. No height too great. No dare untaken. And in the end, we hope, no stone unturned.

Let's take a stroll amongst the carnies, feeling light, so good, your hand in mine. And never mind it's only for tonight. I can make believe; I can pretend. So much the better for reality, but also glad to stop and let it go. To rest awhile somewhere in this mirage.

It could always be so right—so good, just you and me. Escaping from the precipice, so high but so alive. Pay no mind that they're all watching. These spectators of life. The ones who never dare. Forget them all. Forget yourself, and I'll forget you, too. Forget the nevermores, the tragedies we've come to understand and to expect. Lift me up into the light just once before you go. If I fall and hit the ground I promise not to care, only to bleed. And you can join me there. Get lost outside ourselves, the you and me. I think that it's okay if we just ignore it all. Each shifting gaze, the stares of cloudy eyes. The floating and the falling and the demons we all slay.

Cotton candy clouds of Heaven. Toppled popcorn spilt from cardboard boxes coated with a buttery residue, not unlike the feeling of our slipping and tripping along each metal track inside each colorful and light-encrusted vessel. Our chariot awaits. Swing us over and around, through the flavored air. Take us where we've never been before and maybe never want to go again.

We'll still live somewhere between the red and purple lights. Reflections on the dancing carousel. I tried to grab the ring and lost my balance, only to watch myself fall. Thousands of eyes upon me, flashing through each passing mirror. So golden and alive. Like the night of spinning stars, this time will fall away and slide into the past. But we'll remember; maybe each for different reasons, with the pictures that our minds choose to develop. Darkroom happenstance. Overexposure versus too much time to dwell.

I want to remember you for who I thought that you could be. Choose a made-up memory. Forget about the real you, if even just for now. Maybe that's all that will be left after the dissolving. Always spiraling and falling, settling in. Beneath the rubble of the triumph and the setting free of lies. The victory of self. The cleansing and the death of something good.

Either way, I'll miss you when you go.

Virginia Goebel
Poems

Accountable

it was that kind of a day
like a quiet walk in a snowstorm

the misanthrope, the quiescent witness was sure
looked down at all the madness and plucked me out like a
        splinter
"these games are not your games," she said
peeled off my mask and showed me the green face I wore

"I confess," though I balked at my own words
there is no fifth to plead
when life sits red all over your hands

so clear, so vivid those days
endowments gone, invested in shams
every glimmer, every hopeful word, every passion
seeming loneliness leading my hand

pruning myself to hand out as parting gifts
"Do, Do, DO," they'd say on each little note
life is easier to say than to do
though you don't have to say as much to know it

that was my day to listen
to see, to witness, to be
to hold on instead of give away

listening to the referee,
I washed the green,
the sickness, the sadness from my face
I washed the night from my hair
unfolded the face I never thought to wear

it is not an ugly face, it is only mine
just the truth I held at a distance the whole time
the lover, who has guarded her kindness
knowing it's murder to be a crime

I am my only witness
the only keeper of myself

I had to throw away all the "you"s
take back all the missing and the yearning
remove myself from the hunt and the harvest
I dove down, down, down to the bottom of my heart
to have a heart again and call myself a friend

Wounded Birds

listen
do you hear them?

the fierce calls
of the unlikely pairing
of two wounded birds

snarling like teething infants
fighting to remain unseen
to remain in the dark
to hold to the illusions
with such vigor as their wounds allow

they have fooled each other for the nightwings appear
        mended in such lack of light

but
listen as the morning comes
oh that sun comes up
bright and decadent in its revelations

the cooing ends
the passionate echoes die
and they
two birds
two lovers
run

such a simple and ugly thing—
this pride that drives them
an empty and nasty beast

if only they could nestle, nest, wrap necks
with two good wings
two strong wings
they could learn again to fly
revoke their self-imposed banishment from the sky

Inspired by Devon

"Sometimes, at our darkest hour, if we press on, things can
turn out a lot brighter. The trick is not to let it steep too long.
The stronger the tea, the harder it is to sweeten."
—Myma, *A Lighter Shade of Gray* by Devon Pearse.

the should-have-beens sit festering
seeking light, furtively edging from the darkness
towards the door

but today and its imposing misery stand undisputed victors
        of those dreams
leaving only the sweet taste of their memories behind

self-pity, the mark of the lazy mind
a self-imposed torture
of the helpless heart

tap tap tap

a fingernail's tinkling refrain
upon the door
between the heart and the head

there is no climbing out
the door will follow
and the tiniest knocking
the hollowest aching
in the heart that is mocking
your pathetic attempts to drown it

i'm here
i'm still here no matter how you try to poison me

the door shudders

whispertwistturnfightflutter

a spark flies from the spluttering flame within

its burn a faithful reminder that its only true burial will be in
the end

Arm's Length

do not find yourself an irresponsible wretch on my accord

love is a fickle thing
it is everything, yet cold
it drifts through our fingers
the baubles of childhood we could not hold onto
it dances to and fro on your brow
waking you and putting you to bed
love is the shepherd of our irrationalities

so do not buy me a ring

do not follow me to my doom
in the name of love

my dream doesn't include a tribe
or a laughing belly full of you

my heart will take all of you in
and then tire like a harlot
my heart is still somehow a child
unruly and always wanting to be picked up

I must stand guard
I must warn you
when those three words came out they were true
as true as the autumn wind

but truth is always where deceit begins
it is the resting place of the dead
it is the mask that love wears
while sitting on my sleeve

Polar

the two worlds can never consign themselves
wrestling
twirling
snarling
longing
yet ever further
spinning apart

she's a daydream
a sunlit windswept room of soft incense
jazz and tea
spot of coffee
a dabbling of words across the screen
a frolick
a whispered dream
chasing a melody
she is the night's firefly
carrying the daydream
the faith of life's light to the bottom of every bottle
hoping to catch the ray she's missing
to find her daydream again
the crisp sunny day
where her lips will turn aright again

but the night will never bring her back to the daydream
it will only fill her up

with darkness, spite
raging indignation

and he will only be enchanted by the ghost of her light.

Untitled

whispers, unspoken words, dwell in most hearts
occasionally testing their cells, fighting for birth
not unlike a chronic physical malady,
but a special cruelty of the self

intangible, their release never comes
settling on the tongue, breathily, unbidden
teasing but swallowed once again
never making consonance, only diminished vowels

an inconcurrent ooh or aah

fitting not once into the discourse surrounding

given no vehicle, no media, no life
they toil, fight, beg for rationality,
they rebel and surface in the conscious mind like a lightning
        storm
become an ever frequent consumption

resistance becomes survival
circumstances, once chosen, now clung to, allow no
        opportunity
frustration is the cage that fear bought you
no reply can be made to words unspoken

(seldom is seen the scarlet letter that hangs upon the heart)

silence takes the space these words ought to occupy
deafening, blinding, suffocating
rendering incompetent in conversation utterly
leaving nothing but the expected colloquialism

a bitter taste this unjust brew leaves
and mornings woken from dreams that serve as a reminder
show the fault's home, paint its door in red
for words unspoken belong only to the heart in which they lie

Night, Again

it's all for the best, walk away without hesitation
though you know it's better than what you have deserved in
    the past
and better than that which indecision deserves in passing
walk away, the hairs on the back of your neck at attention
the voice inside begging to dig back in
tomorrow you'll quit making me laugh, we'll stop conversing
    like old hats
you'll walk away before the night comes

and then night comes

you walk away in the early morning
in this late leftover night we're left with the same confusion
will it ever change, will we ever grow?
will time take us to another throw of passion
or reel us in for another page in the book of forsaken love
    stories
this game throws me to my knees
I've got no saving throws this time, I'm just as lost as you

our soundtrack plays
in my ears it's just an aria for the wicked
this song yearns for more
a chorus, a bridge, no… a cadence at last
here I sit, with all the uncertainties
looking for an out, or an in, something to define this sin

something to take to lucidity, bring with me to the quasi-
        clarity of morning

but it's all been swallowed
it's at the bottom of the last bottle
and though sobriety has never done me the favor of veracity
so has inebriation done me no favors at all

so where am I at the end of this supposition?
no closer, no further from the authenticity of my heart I trust
but at least a musing has been rendered
a thought has flitted over these ramblings, these ardors
perhaps that's all that I can give
a question with no answer
a rambling consideration with no finale
simply myself at the keyboard in the hours that follow the
        night
wondering where and how I'll be
when the night has ushered me into the morn…

Awake

no one can hear me screaming if I don't let it out
do you, do you, do you know…
guess you couldn't if I've never aired it all out
in clarity, lucidity, away from the bottle that I hide in,
in sanity I have never told you a damn thing that mattered
not that any of this matters, I fell for a dream
amidst the chaos, yours was the smiling face that brought me
        back to myself
but now that I've woken, I can no longer look up and see the
        same sky
it's all gray, and I am like a watercolor
running from the picture but not fast enough for my heart
(it wasn't for you, I wasn't looking for you)
and where am I?
(I wasn't looking to be found)
Can anybody see me? Can anybody feel me?
I love this living thing, I love this seeing thing,
even these tragedies that walk down my face, curve down
        my cheek
and rest on my lips that should be smiling at you
(I used to make you smile)
do you, do you, do you know… just how far I'd go
for that illusion… to bring it with me to the morning
        pillow
for an explanation that didn't make me angry
and I'm fine, yes, I'm fine. I'm always fine, you know.

but what the hell does that really mean? I'm just living and
        breathing.
there is no real sense of peace in that, but who looks any
        further?
but… if I want to live this life, and love this life
and laugh and love and scream,
it's time, I think, though I don't know how, to give up on the
        dream.
after all… knowing you, is really only knowing me when you
        are gone.

Cary Polkovitz
Often Overlooked

I shall miss them.

I shall miss the sound of them. The smells of them.

I would lay on the ground and listen.

My ear pressed against the cool metal. My body against the wooden floorboards. My hip bone invariably too angular and jutting for that to be entirely comfortable but that was part of it. Part of the memory of it.

I would hear the soft sounds from inside.

Towards the end.

The sighing. The quiet swallowing sounds as they ran dry.

Oh it wouldn't start that way. No. It was noisy and it was crude. The banging. The screaming. I often would leave for fear that the noise would drive me mad.

But finally. When things became still. When that first part was over.

That was what I loved.

The soft part. The end. When hope, like the tears, had dried up.

That was when I would return.

And lay there.

And listen as it came to an end.

I hear the sirens now. It won't be long.

I shall miss them.

II

"Whataya think she's doin'?"

Marlene and I sat on the porch that afternoon looking out on the road. It was hot that day. Almost obscenely so. Marlene was a few months older than me. Braces. Red hair. Freckles. She had a habit of wearing a beat-up old Cubbies baseball cap with her ponytail sticking out through the back. I was just starting to get old enough to notice the way her eyes flashed when she had an idea flicker through that odd, little brain of hers and to get a little red in the face when she smiled at me.

We sat on the porch, iced teas making wet rings on the wood that was beginning to show through the balding blue paint. Our baseball cards laid out in front of us. Marlene chewed on her bottom lip as she scanned the cards, her brain figuring which one she wanted to trade for the '76 Vida Blue. My right foot tapped involuntarily, the rubber toecap of my dirty Chuck Taylor drumming rhythmlessly against the inside of the step. Marlene looked up at me, her clear blue eyes showing annoyance at my distracting behavior. Over her shoulder I could see old Mrs Bales shuffling down her flagstone walk to the sidewalk. "Whataya think she's doin'?"

Marlene turned her head sharply and followed my curious gaze. Mrs Bales was wearing her ubiquitous flowered muumuu, her blue hair in its tight curls. In her hand was a beat-up old claw hammer and a rusted-out coffee can. Marlene shifted herself so that she could watch more comfortably. Mrs Bales was old; really old. Well, to us back then she was. You know, the way that older folks can seem to an eleven-year-old on a hot summer afternoon. She moved slowly but deliberately to the old post by the stop sign. The one that, porcupine-like, had nails and screws and other fasteners buried into its soft, dark hide. She put the coffee can under her arm and reached into it extracting a small piece of crumpled paper. She peered at it closely, almost like examining a shopping list, with an almost sad look in her eye. Putting the paper back into the can, Mrs Bales took the claw hammer and pulled a nail off the post and dropped it into the can with a clank. Looking up, she noticed us and waved the can at us in acknowledgement. We smiled and waved back as she methodically made her way back to her house.

A week or so later, Marlene and I were reading comics on the porch. I was acutely aware of my ears tightening when she shuffled closer to point out where the colors on Superman's S were accidentally reversed in the fourth panel of the page we were on. My heart tripped as her shoulder pressed into mine. I buried my head in the comic to look closer, hoping she wouldn't notice that my face had suddenly turned as red as the hero's cape. She suddenly elbowed me in the rib. "Simon," she hissed. "Look. It's Mrs Bales. She's doin' it again."

Looking up, the reprieve from the unfamiliar, nascent emotions surprisingly welcome, my eyes settled on Mrs Bale at the post pulling a screw out of the post this time. She dropped the screw into the old can and walked back to her house, her odd cargo in her left hand. She paused at the bottom step of her porch to adjust the fit of her left stocking before disappearing into the darkness of her house.

Marlene and I spent every afternoon playing together that summer. Some days we saw Mrs Bale at the post (clank).

Sometimes not at all. Marlene had begun to hold my hand when we would walk through the neighborhood, and I noticed that she had begun to wear earrings. We were pretty much inseparable.

On August 3rd, Marlene and I sat on the porch, dressed in our Sunday best. Her blue eyes were red that day and I held her hand in silence. As I recall, that was our first funeral. Marlene's dad had been walking home from work, her family ran the corner soda shop, when a branch from the old elm tree had fallen and cracked his head open on the right side. He hung in for a few days but eventually he threw a clot and died in his sleep. The funeral had been rough and I spent the entirety of it sitting across the way from Marlene as she sobbed on her mother's shoulder.

Mrs Bales shuffled, unnoticed by us down the street with her coffee can and her claw hammer. Halfway back to her house she paused, looked at us and waddled painfully up to my porch. She stopped, her breath coming in soft huffs. She looked down at Marlene with kind rheumy eyes and held her hand out to her. Marlene reached up and Mrs Bales took her small, pale hand into her thin, wrinkled ones. Smiled kindly and softly clucked her tongue. "Here," her voice cracked. "You can watch over him for me. It's only right."

Marlene and I watched as Mrs Bale made her way back to the porch and up the steps and into her house. We looked down at Marlene's hand, still gently gripping whatever it was that the old woman had given her. Opening her hand slowly, Marlene revealed a small, crooked nail, its head bent oddly to the right.

III

C atcher loved stories.

Stories of adventure. Stories of romance. Stories of horror. But mostly stories of wonder. Those stories that left one breathless. The ones that, when you were finished, you put down the book and felt somewhat saddened by leaving a person, a world that had become familiar…almost family.

He would tell the stories to anyone who would listen. Friends, family. Strangers. And people seemed to get something out of his stories. Whether it evoked a feeling, or left one hoping for more. Or…maybe, on those rare occasions, gave them something new to think on. But Catcher had a secret.

Those stories weren't for everyone. Not entirely.

Taking a sip of his coffee, Catcher put the stained mug in the kitchen sink. Tucking his battered old notebook under his arm, he walked quietly out the door of his family home. He lived alone now, in the house his parents (now long gone) passed to him. He walked past the porch where he would sit on the third step and dream up tales. He walked past the mailbox where he would leave chapters for the mailman to pick up and deliver to his editor. He walked past the old tree with the bricks in its roots, looking like the teeth of an old mythological creature, now gnarled and petrified.

Catcher walked three blocks down the road to an old chain-link fence. He pushed his way through the broken links, just as he had done since he was a child.

His feet, clad in their usual tennis shoes, crunched in the dried, unkept lawn as he climbed the slight hill to the old, decrepit house. Its windows boarded up. Its walls beginning to crack and fade with age. Walking around to the back, Catcher found the hole in the wall that he was looking for and sat down. The old, faded green paint flaking off like dead leaves, settling on his shoulders and in his hair.

Inside the house he heard familiar sounds. Footsteps. The rustling of clothing as it was adjusted to make someone more comfortable. The soft padding sound of someone sitting down on the floor just inside.

Lydia.

He could almost feel her warmth through the wall after all this time. This was his audience.

Catcher smiled gently as he opened his notebook and found his newest entry. "In a time, not too long before our own, lived a princess in a tall, tall tower…"

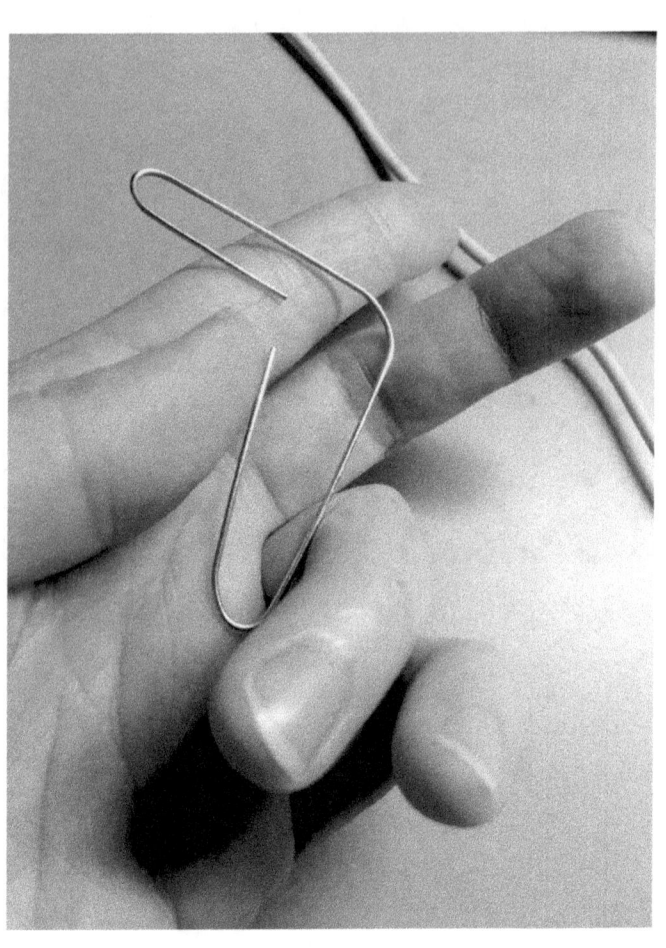

IV

M icah paused. After 23 years, it would soon be over.

One more twist and the game would be finished.

Finding a red paper crane in Baltimore. The sip from the bowl of soup in Arhangay Aymag.

The circle drawn on the chalkboard in the grade school in Nicaragua. The nickel flipped 93 times.

It had been a long journey. He had traveled the world in his quest. Contracting malaria in French Guiana in '98 when he found the blue crayon. Breaking two ribs in Burkina Faso while locating the gum wrapper that had to be turned foil side down. The albino feather plucked from the tail of a dead raven in the Srok Khmer. The toothpick broken directly in half and discarded outside of Ajmer Dargah, Rajasthan.

Arduous was hardly the word for it.

And now…now it was almost over. The adventure was almost finished.

Micah's fingers twitched and he smiled at his own reticence. The smile faded quickly into a look of melancholy as he folded the clip in half.

Photo by Adam Loyal

V

There it was. Franklin couldn't help but let out a gasp.

Its wingspan could be measured in feet. The droplets on its back could fill wading pools.

He had scoffed when his Granny Sadie had told him the story. Walking in the grass one morning, the dew soaking his Keds, he asked her where the water came from.

The Morning Moth, indeed.

The giant thing swiveled its furry head to look squarely at Franklin.

"Well," it said, its voice deep and rumbling and ancient. "Climb aboard. We've got a lot more of this silly old world to cover before the sun rises."

VI

Julianne was 24 and lived in the same house she grew up in. Her room, the room where she had spent her days as a little girl dreaming of the wide world, was still filled with pictures from all over the globe. Africa, the East Indies, Thailand, Australia, Brazil. All her young life she dreamed of travel.

Every day Julianne sat in the same chair at the kitchen table. Twice on weekdays and three times a day on weekends. Every mealtime Julianne sat in the chair with its back to the front door. Her father, a dour man who had recently lost his job as a clerk in the post office downtown not five years earlier, sat quietly drinking his diet cola directly across from her. Her mother, a loving and doting woman, sat in the chair to her left, convenient to the kitchen. The fourth chair was there for when the family would have a guest come by, but tended to be a landing pad for junk mail and newspapers before they went out for the recycling.

Julianne was a surprise for her young parents. They had married only four days earlier when they found out that her mother, an aspiring novelist, was pregnant. Her father had taken a job at the post office as a mail carrier when he found out. It wasn't exactly his dream, but he swore his family would never go hungry. They never did. Life was…well, it was. Julianne grew to be a beautiful young woman, full of life and spirit, her mind carrying her to faraway lands and great adventures. After graduating high school, she took on a job as an assistant librarian downtown to help her family pay the bills. She spent her lunch breaks in the geography section poring over atlases and travel diaries.

Julianne sat in her chair eating a turkey sandwich and reading a book on the island of Rapa Nui when her father put his fork down with a clank against his plate. He folded his newspaper and placed it on the seat to Julianne's right and stood up, his chair scraping the tile floor. Walking to the other side of the table, he took Julianne's hands and stood her up. She watched her father pick up her chair, walk it to the front door and throw it out on to the curb, smashing it to pieces. He then turned to her, took her hands and said one word with a deeply loving smile:

"Go."

The Diner

The diner was completely empty.

Photos of movie stars from the 40s through the late 80s, who had ostensibly visited and partook of the fare, hung crookedly on the white brick walls. Pleather seats with patterned fabric that was never in fashion hugged the walls. Amber light falling on the tables. A failed attempt at… ambience. The soft breathing of the air conditioning almost defining the passage of time.

A feeling of anticipation. Something was about to happen.

"They settled out of court. She had a pretty good case but they settled out of court. He patted her hair remember?" John let out a conspiratorial laugh. The stool by the tiled counter creaked under his weight as he sipped on a glass of diet soda.

Plates clinked as Marion extricated three from the tower on the aluminum counter. Her faded apron, once pink, now grease-stained and threadbare. Her hands gnarled and her feet pained in their black patent leather flats.

Frank stood up from his seat by the table, a half-eaten western omelet left cold and unattended. He walked across the dark carpet, stained with decades of dropped sandwiches, milkshakes and condiments. "Listen," he said. "He's happy, that's what."

Phyllis sipped noisily at her soup spoon. The thick sound breaking the silence for a moment before she paused and looked at the watch she had placed on the table next to her butter knife. She dipped the spoon back into the broth, stirred it and watched the tiny oil slicks reel. "Where's…? Is that fat?"

"That's messed up." Karl said to his companion across from him while he tapped the side of his perspiring water glass. "She didn't even STAY with him." He glowered at his piece of chocolate cake and a piece of icing fell from its precarious perch.

"When's he gonna be here?" John leaned across the counter, his ample gut pressing against it. "Kids is the best," he sighed. "My daughter is 32 now. Kids is the best."

Marion placed a grilled cheese platter and a small tomato juice on an empty table.

"Excuse me?" Frank called out to no one in particular, "Can we sit by the window?"

"Be right back," Karl stated, rising from the table, the chair squeaking against the floor. "Have whatever you want." He circled around to the other side of the table and sat down. He nodded towards the counter. "She's here to look good."

Marion placed a crazed plastic cup on the damp, glossy drain-tray of the soda machine and jerked an orange soda. She watched the door expectantly…almost frightened?

John worked his wallet out of his back pocket and started to leaf through the bills. A twenty. Three tens and five ones. He began to lay them out on the counter. "Hey, you got quarters?"

Marion stared at John with a look lacking any recognition. John shifted uncomfortably. "Where's...uh...Sandy? She owes me a steak."

Frank glanced over at John and Marion. His mouth opened and closed three times in succession. Almost carp-like. "It's ok. I got jealous. Waitaminute. I'm a little worried right now."

Phyllis put her spoon down noisily. She turned in her chair and looked at Frank. She tapped the watch face with the well-manicured nail of her left index finger. The tapping in time with the second hand metronomically.

For a moment there was a pause. The stage was set. The players in their places. A moment where everyone, all at once, forgot their lines. Forgot who they were. Lost in that moment. A feeling of anticipation. Of hope. Of reticence.

The door opened with the smallest of creaks. The diners all turned in their seats. A smile appearing on all faces simultaneously as they saw him in the doorway, the glass door slowly finding its place again behind him; all their expectant faces reflected back at them.

Now they could begin.

About the Contributors

PLAMEN CHETELYAZOV studied at the University of National and World Economy in Sofia and at the University of Plovdiv. In 2005 he participated in the programs for cultural exchange between Bulgaria and the United States of America and spent the summer in Seaside Heights, NJ. Plamen works as a curator and publicist for the Regional History Museum, Plovdiv. Before joining the Museum, he was a probationer at Darik Radio, lifestyle journalist at *Mylife* magazine and an editor at *Anonce* newspaper. His literary pieces have appeared in the magazines *Egoist, Kanape* and the Bulgarian edition of *Glamour*. Plamen is the author of two novels, *Imago* and *Paranoia*, the latter being published in Bulgarian by LiterNet in 2007.

VIRGINIA GOEBEL grew up in sunny Saint Petersburg, Florida, but nobody was surprised when she moved to New York City in 2008. She is a singer-songwriter, actress, poet and prose writer. Her work has been published by *Tasco Magazine* and *vanquer.net* as well as *Stetson Reporter* where she served as Assistant Life Editor and weekly column writer. Virginia may usually be found in her Bronx apartment, guitar in hand, singing and creating.

Born and raised a Florida girl, DEVON PEARSE cherishes the inevitable inspiration brought on by nature, sunlight and particularly water. Her family is filled with readers and writers of poetry, prose, short stories, and anything they're inspired by. From an early age, Devon learned to love, respect and honor many celebrated (and not-so-celebrated) writers and poets, and her greatest desire is to meet them one day in the Great Beyond and have them say of her writing, "That wasn't half bad!" Devon is the author of *A Lighter Shade of Gray*, a semi-autobiographical though also fictionalized novel, released by Neverland Publishing in 2010, and her second novel, *The Untrodden Ways*, will be released…someday. She currently resides in a colorful townhouse filled with creativity, art, inspiration, daydreams, and love.

Cary Polkovitz likes to tell stories. Born in Port Jefferson, NY, he went to school for Illustration and Design at Pratt Institute in Brooklyn, NY. Cary has published two volumes of creative vignettes under the title *Often Overlooked* and is currently working on two graphic novels, *UKIYO* and *Meaning But Without the Words*. He has been a cartoonist, a graphic designer, a bartender, an art teacher and a painter. Cary lives in Florida with his wife, a chestnut squirrel, a bird and a three-legged cat.

James Wilson is the author of two volumes of prose poems, *All the Colours Fade* and *The Song Remains the Same* (both Miami, FL: The Hippocrene Society, 2012) and the essay collection *Images of the Afterlife in Cinema* (London: Duchy of Lambeth, 2011). His debut novel, *Three Bridges*, was issued by Neverland Publishing in 2014. James is also the translator of two volumes of the French writer Guy de Maupassant: *To the Sun* and *The Foreign Soul & The Angelus* and his prose fiction has appeared in the journals *The Use of English* and *Snow*. He lives in London where he works as an editor and librarian for the Swedenborg Society.